That Kind of Woman
The Life and Career of Barbara Nichols

Richard Koper

BearManor Media

Albany, Georgia

That Kind of Woman: The Life and Career of Barbara Nichols
Copyright © 2016 Richard Koper. All Rights Reserved.

No part of this book may be reproduced in any form or by any means, electronic, mechanical, digital, photocopying or recording, except for the inclusion in a review, without permission in writing from the the publisher.

Published in the USA by
BearManor Media
P.O. Box 71426
Albany, GA 31708
www.BearManorMedia.com

Softcover Edition
ISBN-10: 1-62933-079-5
ISBN-13: 978-1-62933-079-2

Printed in the United States of America

Table of Contents

Acknowledgements   vii
Foreword by John K. Carpenter   ix
Introduction   xvii

Biography
 Ancestry   1
 Teenage Vixen   17
 Career Girl   31
 Breakthrough   55
 Movie Star   73
 The King and the Girl from Queens   93
 The Sweet Smell of Success   105
 Nichols versus Mansfield, Monroe, and Novak   121
 Casualty and Recognition   133
 That Kind of Woman   151
 TV Star and Acclaim   167
 Who Was That Lady?   185
 Women in Love   201
 Losing Grip   217
 Comedy and Science Fiction   227
 Decline   247
 Health Problems   263

Filmography   281
 River of No Return   281
 Manfish   282
 Miracle in the Rain   282
 The Wild Party   283
 Beyond a Reasonable Doubt   283
 The King and Four Queens   283
 Sweet Smell of Success   284
 The Pajama Game   284
 Pal Joey   285
 Ten North Frederick   285
 The Naked and the Dead   286
 That Kind of Woman   286
 Woman Obsessed   287
 The Scarface Mob   287
 Who Was That Lady?   288

Where the Boys Are	288
The George Raft Story	288
House of Women	289
The World of Henry Orient	289
Looking for Love	290
Dear Heart	290
The Disorderly Orderly	291
The Human Duplicators	291
The Loved One	292
The Swinger	292
The Power	293
Sette Uomini e un Cervello	293
Charley and the Angel	294
The Photographer	294
Won Ton, the Dog Who Saved Hollywood	295
Television Appearances	323
Magazine Covers	355
Bibliography	383
Index	385

Acknowledgments

IN LOVING MEMORY OF MISS GLORIA PALL. She was very helpful in telling the stories she remembered very vividly from her days as a pin-up girl and starlet in New York and Hollywood. A wonderful, kind and sharing woman. You are missed.

Many thanks to Janice L. Pease and John K. Carpenter, two of Barbara's relatives, who were so kind to talk to me about their first and second cousin. Thank you Janice for the use of your rare photographs from Barbara's private collection, and thank you, John, film historian and lecturer of classic film programs, for writing the book's Foreword.

Many thanks to: John Tierney, for letting me use the pictures that a young Barbara gave to his dad; John Cohan, for sharing his memories and saucy stories of his former client with me; Bruce Blau, for his help and sending me the pictures from his mother's memorabilia; Kathleen Hughes, a wonderful and friendly lady; Paula Stewart, for talking with me about her long-time friendship with Barbara and contacting her ex-husband, the late Jack Carter for me; Elaine Hollingsworth, who worked under her stage name, "Sara Shane," with Barbara; Christopher Riordan, for all his help and sharing the wonderful stories of his younger days in Hollywood; The very friendly Tab Hunter, who was so nice to grant me a telephone interview; Ron Russell—what a wonderful story he shared with me; Dennis Holmes, such a friendly man, who worked with Barbara when he was a kid; Shirley Knight, a wonderful lady—I'm very proud she shared her memories with me; Mamie Van Doren—I wish her much success in writing her own book about her sexy contemporaries; Peter Ford, what a hilarious story he told me. He took the time to talk to me admits his home renovations; Margaret Teele, a friendly lady and very helpful telling me her memories on working with Barbara; William B. Hillman, a positive and friendly person. He shared a rather sad story that shows Barbara's vulnerability but at the same time her strength and humor; James Krajewski, for letting me use two photos and several magazine covers from his collection.

Also thank you very much for being so friendly to talk with me or responding to my e-mails: Elaine Cox, Tom Fitzpatrick, Conrad Janis, Maria-Flora Smoller, Michael Dante, Melinda Markey, James Best, Ray Strait, Dyanne Thorne, Marvin Kaplan, Mimi Gibson, Marlyn Mason, Robert Bouvard, Santiago Rodriguez, Lauren Angelich, Rob Matteson, Taylor Pero, Franco Corridoni, Barbara Luna, Kathleen Cody, and Michael B. Druxman.

Acknowledgments

Last but not least, I would like to thank my revisor, Patricia Prud'homme van Reine, for all her help with proofreading and revising my manuscript.

(Photo courtesy of James Krajewski).

Foreword

by John K. Carpenter

ONE OF THE SADDEST THINGS in my life is that I never had the opportunity to meet my second cousin, Barbara Nichols. My father, Bert, who grew up with her, was the same age, and shared creative endeavours of singing and performing with local bands and on the stage, spoke to me of Barbara's drive, determination, and personality all through my growing up. He said to me that had Barbara ever had the chance to meet me and just see how much I was addicted to the same theatrical and entertainment ambitions, she would steal me away; that she would take me under her wing and try to adopt me from him! I grew up hearing about my second cousin Barbara so much from my dad, my grandmother Viola, and grandfather Egbert Carpenter, that I not only felt as though I knew her but that I was meant to be in the same entertainment career as she was.

In their stories, I heard an underlying sense of sadness that, no matter how widely-known her name was, she missed the fact that she never could settle down and have a family of her own. This is why it was taken as a matter of fact that she would love and adore me and want me as her own. As I recently heard in a rare TV interview she gave, while on the publicity route to promote her triumph dramatic performance in *Sweet Smell of Success*, she was always engaged in work, but never engaged for marriage.

Barbara was alone in her career, did it all, and got there all by herself. Her looks, voluptuous figure, seductive face, and manner were tools that she learned to use for her own benefit. Hearing her talk about her career, and how the family would speak of her, I could tell that, in essence, she was a star but also an outcast, who hid her emptiness in her determination and character, which typecast her in an era when the dumb street savvy blonde was going out of style.

I understand her emotions, due to my own ambition and determination, qualities that further reminded my father and his parents of Barbara. She was nothing like the easily-taken-advantage-of character that she portrayed in musicals, dramas, and comedies. Barbara was an educated, savvy, New York gal, who wanted to shed her beginnings (being born from an unwed mother—my aunt Julia—who married my uncle, George Nickerauer), and get the respect of her family by overcoming these initial boundaries that made her less than decent in those days.

Barbara was wild, though, and my father was heard saying how she was always running around half-naked. She shared a common bond with my then band-singer father, which made his own mom constantly worry that the two would have sex and have a child. This was prejudice that came from her being the child of an unwed mother. Typecasting herself was a smart choice to be continuously cast, but it branded her as a dumb blonde with street sense, and not the girl you'd bring home to meet mother! This led to her increased drinking, which, in turn, led to car accidents and even falling off the stage during a performance and hurting her leg.

Hollywood never changes, and sex always has and always will sell the product. Barbara used this to secure a busy work schedule and always keep in demand, but as my father told me: sex was also how the studio or managers could control you, if not outright own you.

As a singer, my father informed me how he was offered recording contracts if he would be the lover to a top mob kingpin, an offer that made him drop out of the game, even when so many others he knew took advantage of the offer. Barbara was told to avoid becoming pregnant or she would lose her contract (a similar thing Jean Harlow was told by Louis B. Mayer). The starlets were investments that could not lose their appeal. Barbara did not want to give up all she had given up so much for, so she chose to follow the plan, an aspect of what saddened her future deeply.

Having starred on the New York stage, and being a theatrically shown independent filmmaker myself, I can say from experience that no matter how great the success or the achievement at making your dreams become your realities, going through each success alone is an empty, bottomless void that, despite endless searching, usually never fills up. I feel this was Barbara's situation. On screen, she was every man's heartthrob, but in reality her determination made her a one-woman work horse.

She was a fantastic actress, especially since the character she portrayed was nowhere near the great happy, peppy, and smart career woman she truly was! I felt that keeping her memory alive as a fantastic actress and sex kitten was to be my purpose for being like her in so many career-minded ways—to keep the talent in the family, so to speak. She has been my own personal inspiration, and the person to live up to.

Now, here's Mr Koper's magnificent book on my grand and glorious cousin, Barbara Nickerauer aka Barbara Nichols, and I honestly feel that proper representation of the major talent she was has finally been given to her.

THAT KIND OF WOMAN

Pin Up photo, 1951.

Picturegoer magazine, November 30, 1957.

Barbara in *The Disorderly Orderly*, 1964.

Foreword

(Photo courtesy of James Krajewski).

Introduction

AFTER WORLD WAR II, BARBARA MARIE NICKERAUER had developed into a strikingly beautiful young lady, a good-looking teenager, who felt the vibrations of new possibilities and the exciting and promising times that lay ahead. Growing up close to New York City, in the protective environment her German mother provided, Barbara was a headstrong girl, who wanted more out of life than being someone's girlfriend and wife. She entered beauty contests and modelled clothes for shows and department stores on Long Island. Due to her modeling jobs, Barbara had visited the city her mother warned her about a couple of times, and she fell in love with it.

New York was buzzing with activity. By the late 1940s, the city had become the world's largest manufacturing center. The garment district occupied eighteen blocks of loft buildings bounded by 34th and 40th Street and Sixth and Ninth Avenue. Undergarment manufacturing took place downtown, along lower Broadway. A lot of pretty girls were needed to model and help sell the clothes and undergarments that were manufactured.

In December 1946, the United Nations selected New York as the location for its permanent headquarters, thus making New York City the capital of the world. Along with the economic boom came an exciting cultural boost. In 1947, Maurice Chevalier and Edith Piaf gave concerts on Broadway. Famous musical shows that were put on that year were *Brigadoon*, *Oklahoma!*, and *Finian's Rainbow*. Many fashion models held jobs as showgirls in these musicals, as well.

At the time, a popular song on the radio stations was "I'm Gonna Be a Bad Girl," written and sung by Monica Lewis. Its refrain encouraged young girls to get the most out of life and not wait at home to be asked for marriage:

"I'm gonna be a bad girl, I'll shock the neighborhood.
and brother as a bad girl, I'm gonna be good.
I'm gonna be a bad girl, I'm gonna learn to drink.
I'm gonna wear my man out and then I'll wear mink.
I'm gonna be a playgirl, I'm gonna be a witch.
And then someday I'll marry, a son of a rich."

One can imagine the young and good-looking Barbara taking these lyrics to heart. She must have decided there and then that she wanted more out of life than what her parents had envisioned for their only child. In December 1947, she flew to the Caribbean to dance in a floor show at several prestigious hotels. Once she returned to the United States, there was no turning back. Twenty-year-old Barbara packed her bags and moved to Manhattan. Now a blonde, she worked as a model by day and as a showgirl at several niteries in the evening. After work, she stepped out on the town and had fun.

Another blonde on the New York scene, who eventually made a name for herself in the mid-1950s, was Gloria Pall (1927-2012). A native of the

Big Apple, Gloria had met and worked with Barbara on a modeling job and experienced her career obsession and animosity towards her competition.

In Hollywood, Gloria had several encounters with Barbara again. She said, "I was always friendly with everyone. Only problem was Jayne Mansfield and Barbara Nichols out of hundreds. The most miserable one of all was Barbara Nichols. I know she died young from Cirrhosis. She was a big boozer!"[1]

Modeling had become quite a lucrative job for Barbara and she was soon a favorite in the men's magazines of the day. In 1948, she appeared on the cover of *See* magazine. Inside, there were pictures of Barbara next to a young Marilyn Monroe. Both girls were modelling sensations on different shores. Barbara was an east coast model, while Marilyn was a movie starlet on the west coast.

Barbara recalled later, "I became a model for bathing suits and cheesecake shots. This appealed to me more than fashion modelling because they like curves, not flat chests. All my movie roles, like the one I have in *Sweet Smell of Success*, have called for a full figure, too."

The late 1940s marked the start of nationwide television broadcasting. The big broadcasting stations were stationed in New York City. Barbara entered the TV world in 1951. She immediately made sure she was noticed by the public, which eventually resulted in the fact that she and the shows she appeared on were taken off the air.

When she was cast in a small nonspeaking part in the stage musical *Pal Joey* on Broadway, Barbara solemnly told columnist Earl Wilson it didn't bother her. "In many musicals, the girls with the best lines never say a word."

In 1955 Barbara was offered the leading part of a dumb blonde actress in the stage play, *Will Success Spoil Rock Hunter?* She said no to the offer. Instead, she was cast by Warner Bros. Studios for *Miracle in the Rain*. The movie was filmed on location in New York City. On a night out at Sardi's, Barbara met Hollywood producer Bert Friedlob. He needed a sexy blonde for his new movie. They wined and dined and then it got quiet. Barbara quickly forgot about the meeting. "I forgot it, because they always look at everybody in New

---

[1] Source: email contact with author.

York and hire somebody in Hollywood." Eventually, Barbara left New York for Hollywood.

In Hollywood, Barbara profiled herself as a comedienne in TV shows with Jack Benny and Red Skelton, but was also sought for when a part required more dramatic input. The mid-1950s shaped her as a character actress and showed her true talent as a comedienne and strong dramatic actress. Her roles in *Sweet Smell of Success* and *That Kind of Woman* showcase her acting ability. She could have—and in retrospective, should have—been cast in more roles of the same calibre, as in the movies mentioned above.

An unnamed reader of *Modern Screen* movie magazine sent in a letter in March 1958 asking, "Marilyn Monroe, Jayne Mansfield, Barbara Nichols, and Mamie Van Doren along with Marie Wilson have been typed as 'dumb blondes.' Which of these girls is the smartest and which has the most talent?" To which the editor of *Modern Screen* answered: "Probably Nichols."

In 1960, *People Today* magazine called Barbara their "People's Pet" and wrote in the small accompanying article, "Unlike other Hollywood actresses who have been acclaimed for their talent, lovely Barbara Nichols doesn't pretend to be the *grande dame* of the theatre. Says bosomy Barbara: 'I like fun too much to be stiff and formal. A snob can't enjoy herself—unless she just enjoys being a snob.' Barbara Nichols likes to be herself at all times, and it is this attitude that has made her one of the most popular people in the movie colony. Her friends range from top stars to grips, gaffers and script girls—all say they have never met a warmer, less affected, more genuine person. Neither have we."[2]

While researching Barbara's life and career, and through talking with many people who knew her well and worked with her, I found confirmation of *People Today's* description of Barbara. For example, I quote actor Tab Hunter, who worked with her in *That Kind of Woman*. "She was a really good actress. There was something kind of wonderful about her; you just wanted to put your arms around her. Very lovable, very vulnerable. I always liked her quality.

[2] *People Today*, August 1960.

Quality is very important. She projected just a lovely demeanor, you know, that you wanted to know more about her."[3]

In the early 1960s, Barbara's career thrived. She did a lot of TV and had guest starring roles in several A-list comedies. 1950s child actress Mimi Gibson met Barbara on the set of Westinghouse Playhouse's TV show, *House Guest*, in 1961. Gibson said, "She was terrific as a dumb blonde, but dumb she was not. I was a kid and we really didn't talk to each other that much, but one always admired people who find their niche. She did and made a good living from it. I remember someone telling my mom she was a good businesswoman."[4]

In 1961, Barbara returned to the Broadway stage. Columnist Earl Wilson asked her if she made a lot of money when doing *Let It Ride!* She answered, "That's not from here honey. I did two pictures back-to-back. I make a lot of money every week. Some television shows can't afford me."[5]

Within the movie and film industry, Barbara established herself as a reliable, friendly and hardworking laborer. Because of her professionalism, people such as Desi Arnaz, producer for Desilu TV studios, and many other casting directors, producers, and directors, regularly called on her services.

Barbara never married. She had to support herself. She had to pay her own bills, and working regularly meant a steady income. She loved to paint and cook for family and friends. She lived with her pets, and they kept her company.

Her cousin, Janice Pease, visited Barbara regularly in the 1960s. She recalled a funny incident that occurred around 1965 with one of Barbara's dogs. "Barbee Girl was not a fan of mine, when I went to sleep with Barb in her bed, she snarled and bared her teeth. I slept on the couch. The second bedroom didn't have a bed; it was full of portable closets full of clothes. She told me they would come back in style—and she was correct."[6]

---

[3] Source: telephone conversation with author, 11-17-2015.

[4] Source: email contact with author.

[5] *Beaver County Times*, January 6, 1962.

[6] Source: email contact with author.

Apart from being a place of glorification and fame, Hollywood is also known as a place of disillusion and hardship. When an actress gets older and fights hard to resist the loss of her youth, she can feel unwanted and old when only thirty years old. Barbara tried to laugh at this and kept believing her persona and charisma would pull her through and secure other career opportunities. Nevertheless, she fell victim to this skewed view of aging, too, and was without work most of the time during the late 1960s and 1970s.

In one of Barbara's last movies, she worked with director William Byron Hillman. Hillman experienced Barbara's decline and survivor's mentality at the same time. "Barbara told a pile of stories every day," he said. "Some of the info was personal and should not be repeated by me third person. I loved her stories and believe each one. Heard some great secrets that need to remain just that—a secret. She loved to laugh and even when troubled found time to talk about flubbed lines or how she loved to tease or surprise her fellow cast and crew. She found a way to do this every day, and regardless of her demons, she enjoyed life. As for her drinking: I think it started slowly at parties, casual drinks that just increased over time and soon got out of hand. Happens to lots of people, famous or not. I don't think it was from depression or health problems. Babs was a healthy fun lady who drank and at times drank too much. I know in the end, the drink did her in and destroyed her kidneys. That's the saddest part of her journey. We all get older and some hate the changes. The drink seems to mentally help that but sadly it doesn't. By the time you realize the drink is killing you it's too late. That was Barbara's story. It just happened. Always fun to be the life of the party until the life dims."[7]

This book is a tribute to the actress Barbara Nichols, who illuminated the movie and TV scenes she was in. Although her private life may have been troubled at times, to this day she is remembered as the wisecracking, vulnerable, not so dumb blonde she portrayed so well.

---

[7] Source: email contact with author.

Introduction

Model Agency Card, 1949.

THAT KIND OF WOMAN

Model Agency Card, 1949.

Introduction

Signed photo. (Photo courtesy of Janice Pease).

TV Show magazine, January 1952.

Barbara on Jamaica, 1955. (Photo courtesy of Janice Pease).

That Kind of Woman

Barbara in her dressing room at Warner Bros., 1955.

INTRODUCTION

Lobby card for *Beyond a Reasonable Doubt*, 1956.

Barbara on the set of *Sweet Smell of Success* with columnist Sidney Skolsky, 1957.

Warner Bros. Pin Up photo, 1957.

Barbara and Gary Cooper in *Ten North Frederick*, 1958.

Dinner with friends, circa 1970.

Introduction

Barbara and Army Archerd at the *Won Ton Ton* Wrap Party, 1976.

BIOGRAPHY

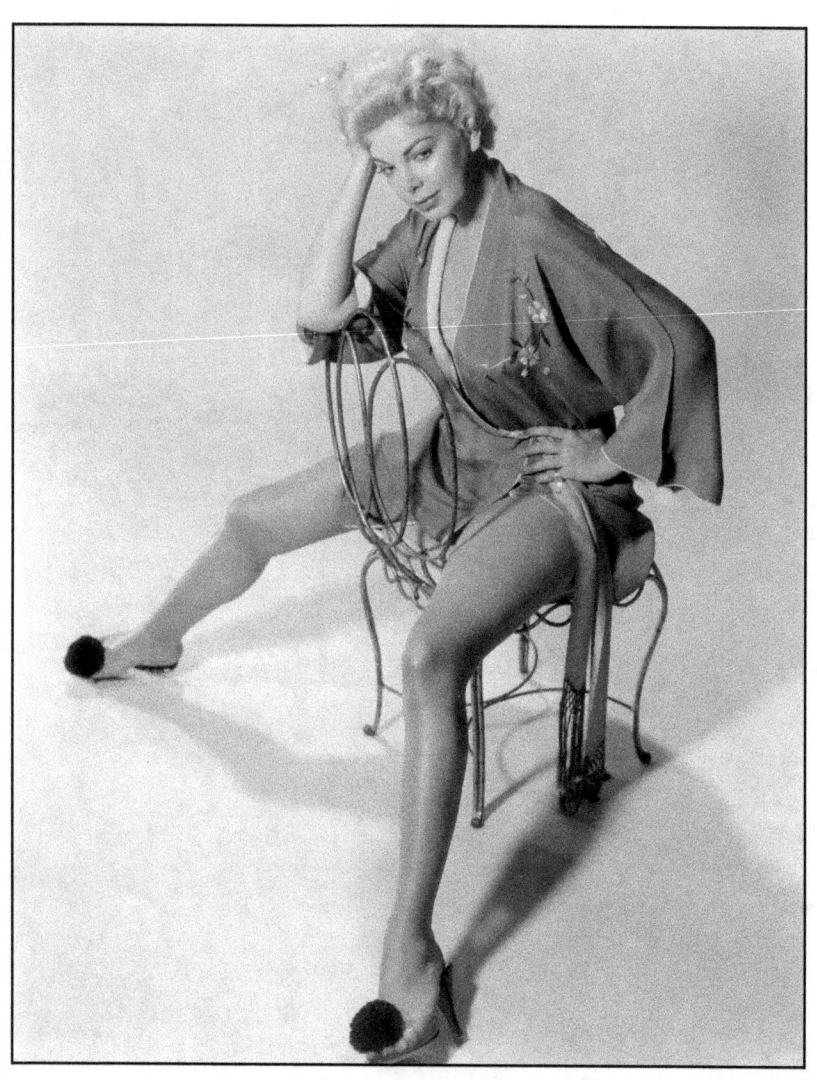

Ancestry

BARBARA NICHOLS WAS BORN as Barbara Marie Nickerauer in Mineola on Long Island, New York, on December 10, 1928. The village is situated in Nassau County, New York, and the name is derived from a Native American word meaning "pleasant place." Barbara is registered as the daughter of Julia—sometimes called Julie—Marie Nickerauer-Wurst (b. April 3, 1906) and George A. Nickerauer (b. July 2, 1908). He married Julia a year and a half after Barbara's birth. George wasn't Barbara's biological father, but Barbara did always consider him as her father.

George Nickerauer grew up at Broadway and Vine in Manhattan, with his mother Louise Nickerauer-Seidenburg and father George Adam

Nickerauer (b. May 12, 1877). George Sr. was employed as a carpenter at the United States Army aviation field of Mineola. Some of the most famous pilots in American history flew from Mineola's aviation field. In 1927, for instance, Charles Lindbergh started his historic flight to Paris from nearby Roosevelt Field.

When their youngest daughter died suddenly on July 13, 1915, Louise and George were devastated. Three-year-old Gertrude Nickerauer died from injuries and burns received when she was playing with matches and her dress caught on fire. Because of the loss of his daughter, George's drinking habits intensified, causing a lot of stress within his family.

In September of 1917, nine-year-old George, his mother Louise, and his three siblings—Viola, Ruth, and August—were dispossessed of their home at 71 Rockaway Road and lived in straitened circumstances, because George Sr. was in Raymond Street jail, Brooklyn. He was held on a bail of $1,000, awaiting the action of the Federal Grand Jury.

With no money to feed her children, Louise lived in a two-room apartment on Jamaica Avenue, near Beach Street, Richmond Hill. Thomas F. Tevlin, George's lawyer, found the family in starving conditions and arranged funds to give Louise and her four children some temporary aid. Due to his detention, George Sr. had lost his job as a carpenter at Camp Upton, Yaphank. Tevlin tried to interest charitable persons in providing bail for his client so he would be able to support his family again.

George Sr. had been accused of buying liquor for soldiers in uniform. In his defence he stated that he had bought the liquor for himself and family, as was his custom. When he came out of the saloon where he had bought the liquor, a Patrolman stopped him to inquire what he had wrapped up in a paper bundle. When George Sr. informed the officer that it was beer, the policeman called him a bum and he was struck over the head. The policeman continued to strike him over the legs and body until he was badly bruised. The soldiers standing by made inquiry as to where George Sr. lived and voluntarily gave their names to his wife, so that they could appear as witnesses for him in court. With the help of these soldiers' testimonies, George Sr. was released from all charges and set free after a couple of months in detention.

Almost a year after his release, he left to fight in World War One. He was sent to Europe in 1918, to join France and England in their fight against the German army. The United States were almost completely unprepared to participate in the war. The manpower and supplies needed to field an expeditionary force were at the lowest since the Civil War. When the bloody and cruel war ended on November 11, 1918, a wounded, traumatized, and disillusioned George Sr. returned home to his wife and children. His drinking worsened over the years, and on January 7, 1939, when Barbara was ten years old, George Sr. died from a lingering illness at the age of sixty-one.

Barbara's great-grandfather, Adam Nickerauer, was born in Germany and came to the United States in 1867. Once a soldier, he became a veteran of the Civil War. Her great-grandmother, Adelia, died in 1917. Adam Nickerauer died on December 28, 1927, eighty-two years old, at his house in Jamaica.

Three and a half years after his grandfather's death, George's older brother, August, was sentenced to two to four years' imprisonment when he was found guilty of manslaughter in the second degree. August Nickerauer went on trial on June 30, 1931 for being the operator of a car that crashed into another car on May 30, killing two women. His drunken driving, and the fact that he denied he had driven the car and found a friend to lie for him in court, didn't help his case. John Carpenter, the son of Barbara's cousin Egbert Carpenter, mentions that, although he was innocent, his "uncle Gussie" took the blame for the murder. Mafia kingpins promised to support him for life—and they did, for August never had to work again. He lived with an Italian family in their basement until he died.

The Nickerauer women were strong-willed ladies. Starting with their mother Louise, who was a dominant and strong woman, George's two sisters were to be reckoned with also. John Carpenter remembered his grandmother Viola, George's sister, dancing the Charleston on the table with her husband, during family meetings. Alcoholism ran through the entire family, as in the Depression Era, life was tough, and some joy and relief from everyday stress could be found in liquor. Although Barbara was very fond of her parents and they stayed close to each other until her death, in her later years during the sessions with her psychic John Cohan, she confided that hers was a dysfunctional family. Cohan recalled her saying that in her family "that drinking problem" was in full bloom.

Barbara's mother was born in the small village of Wolfenbrück, Baden-Württemberg, in the South of Germany. As a young girl, she experienced the horrors of World War One and saw the shame and humiliation that her parents and other adults experienced when Germany lost the war. The country was in total chaos and many Germans were preparing to leave the country to find a better living in "the land of the free," the United States of America.

A 1954 newspaper article mentioned that Julia's eighty-two-year-old father, Johann Wurst, still lived in Germany and her brother Carl lived with his wife, Angelica, and daughters, Eileen and Carol, in Great Neck, New York. Julia's brother, Emil, also lived close by on Long Island. Another brother, Fritz Wurst, lived in Florida, and Julia's two sisters, Maria Dias and Roselle Linke, lived in Germany. Julia was close to her family, even though she never returned to Germany to visit them.

Petite, generously endowed Julia, and her brothers, Carl and Emil, arrived in the United States around 1925. Happy to start a new life, Julia was a fun girl, who set out to enjoy life. She found a job as a cook/maid for a rich Long Island family, and her life couldn't have been better. The chauffeur of the family took a liking to the German girl with the broken accent. When he got her pregnant and wouldn't marry her, Julia had to find a man who wanted to support her and would be a father for her child, too. Abortion was not an option for her, not only because it was illegal and many women died in the procedure, but mainly because she loved children. She met twenty-year-old George Nickerauer, and in him she found a willing candidate to date and eventually marry her after the baby was born.

George and Julia were officially married on April 30, 1930. Their marriage license was registered in May 1930. George proved to be a reliable husband and father. In 1935, the family bought a house on 15120 Goldfield

Street at 151st Avenue in South Ozone Park, Queens, New York. George was a member of the Democratic Party, at the time. The 1940 census of The Department of Commerce mentions that Barbara's father is working as a mechanic, his working class is stated as "employer" with a yearly income of $800. George was a hard worker, having experienced hunger and poverty during his youth. He made sure his wife and daughter would never have to experience his ordeals.

Ten-year-old Barbara and her parents visited New York's World's Fair of 1939-1940 at Flushing Meadows and Corona Park, and were amazed by all the wonderful expositions, shows, and exhibitions. The young girl was especially enchanted with the spectacular musical and water extravaganza presented at The Billy Rose Aquacade. The cost of admission was 80¢. The show was presented in a special amphitheatre seating 10,000 people and included an orchestra to accompany the spectacular synchronized swimming performance. It featured Johnny Weismuller and Eleanor Holm, two of the most-celebrated swimmers of the era, and dazzled fairgoers with its lighting and cascades and curtains of water, pumped in waterfalls at 8,000 gallons a minute. Barbara was afraid of swimming, but for weeks to come, she dreamed of becoming a glamorous star.

In 1942, Barbara's parents decide to move from South Ozone Park to 116-39th Street, Jamaica. Jamaica was a middle-class neighborhood in the New York borough of Queens. George, the breadwinner, owned a gas station on Baisley Boulevard called Rauer's. George's brother-in-law, Ruth's husband, Harold Siedenburg was a businessman that owned several garages in and around New York. He provided George with a steady job managing the gas station. The Nickerauers lived in a semi-detached house with an enclosed front porch, a living room, dining room, and kitchen all in a line, and three bedrooms and a bath upstairs. Most houses in Ozone Park and Jamaica were built roughly to the same plan.

With the country's involvement in World War Two, Julia applied to become a naturalized American citizen in 1942. Up until then, she had retained her German citizenship. Because of the Alien Registration Act of

1940, Julia decided to apply for US citizenship. The Roosevelt government passed a bill that allowed the FBI to investigate citizens of German descent. People were questioned, and houses were searched in order to find out if these people were actually Nazi spies or showed sympathy for Adolf Hitler. If they were found guilty, they were taken from their homes and interned into camps. Some were even sent back to Germany, a country they'd left in their childhood or had never been to at all.

Julia and her brother, Carl, were afraid that some neighbor would point them out as a threat to the United States. Luckily, George was considered a true American, and the fact that he had a Jewish mother also was to their advantage. Nevertheless, the anxiety and fear of her parents must have been felt by then eleven-year-old Barbara, when the *New York Times* wrote an article titled "FBI tightens curb on 256,000 aliens":

"City policemen, FBI officials admitted yesterday, are engaged in a check-up of 256,000 aliens of enemy nations in this city ... Detectives and other city operatives will visit every person who registered. In such case they will check home and business address, daily activity and routine ... Dossiers will be made of all aliens of enemy nations, natives of Germany, Italy, Japan, and their lesser allies. The records will check also on the number of persons in each family and on the whereabouts of each member of the family ... The police check-up and dossier system here is only the beginning of a more intensive watch of aliens. The same movement is to spread into adjoining counties such as Nassau, Suffolk, Westchester and Rockland and eventually throughout the whole States."[8] Much to her relief, Julia obtained the American nationality on August 22, 1944.

Barbara's mother was a typical homemaker and she disliked to travel. Her parents led a quiet life on Long Island. Barbara later remarked, "I was born on Long Island and never got to Brooklyn because my mother told me it was just like visiting a foreign country."

Barbara's cousin, Janice Pease, described her uncle and aunt: "Julia was a total homebody. She was also very involved in the Lutheran church. George

[8] *The New York Times*, April 1, 1942.

was my mother's brother. He was a carpenter and sanitation engineer. He was the original re-cycler, I remember he had stacks of sorted materials in his garage, cardboard, newspapers. Bound in neat piles."[9]

Barbara was the apple of her mother's eye. Julia spoiled her only child. Barbara didn't need to do many household chores, but Julia did teach her daughter how to bake pastry and cook gourmet meals. Barbara was a pretty girl and when she reaches puberty she started getting the attention from the boys in her neighbourhood. George wasn't too pleased with this, but Julia encouraged Barbara to walk straight and show off her lovely physique. In her early teens, Julia sent Barbara to dancing school to develop her body and give her poise. Barbara recalled later, "It helped so much that when I was sixteen I won a bathing beauty contest. After that, I knew the stage would be my career, there was no turning aside."

---

[9] Source: email contact with author.

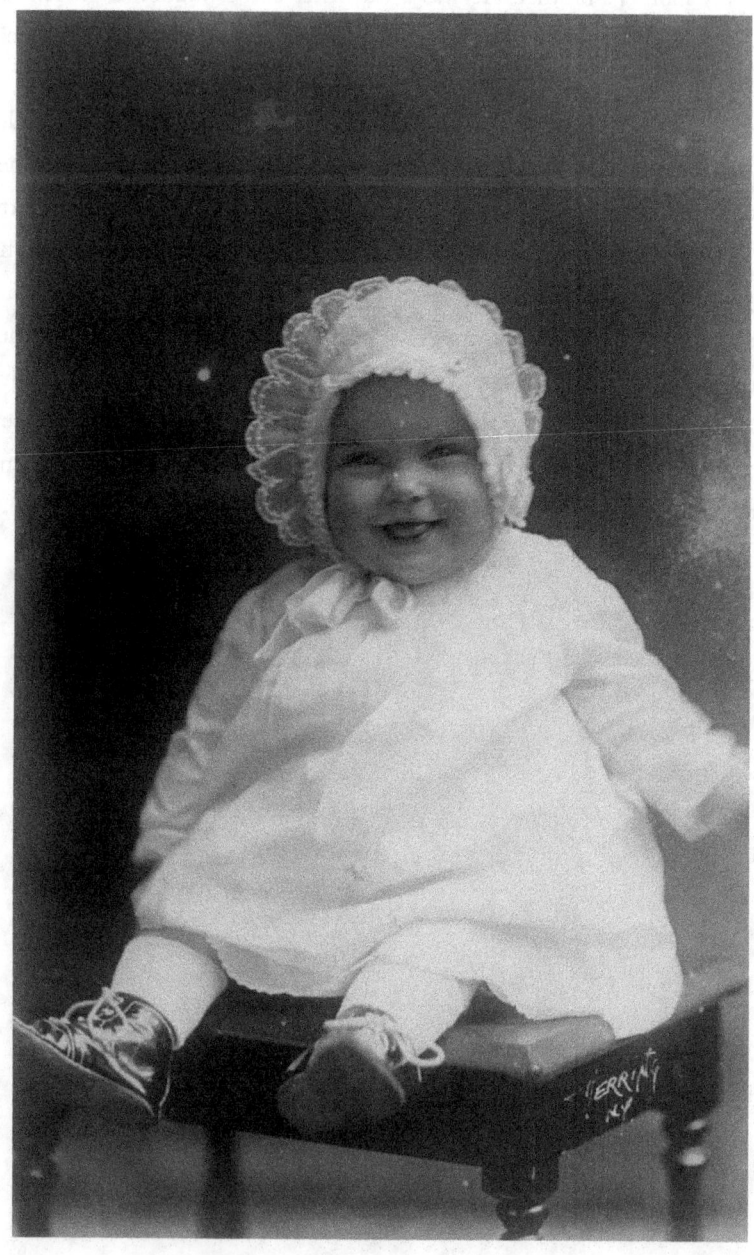

Baby Barbara. (Photo courtesy of Janice Pease).

Julia Wurst - second from the right - waves as she arrives in the United States. (Photo courtesy of Janice Pease).

Julia and baby Barbara. (Photo courtesy of Janice Pease).

George Nickerauer, circa 1926. (Photo courtesy of Janice Pease).

Barbara and neighborhood friend Henry, circa 1938.
(Photo courtesy of Janice Pease).

Barbara at the New York World's Fair, 1939. (Photo courtesy of Janice Pease).

Barbara in her parent's backyard, circa 1940.

Barbara and a friend in front of church, circa 1941. (Photo courtesy of Janice Pease).

Barbara as a bobbysoxer, circa 1942.

Teenage Vixen

IN 1942, BARBARA WAS A FIRST GRADER at Woodrow Wilson High School. A 1956 magazine article mentions that she wasn't much interested in school. "With the aid of adoring acolytes who did her homework for her and slipped her correct answers for exams, Barbara scraped through school."[10] This proved to be far from the truth. Maybe Barbara lost her interest when she got older, but her early report cards show us an A+ student. Her report card from the first grade (September 1942-July 1943) shows excellent marks and an A for conduct. Her teacher, E. F. Proctor, remarks on the back that Barbara is doing very well at school. Three years later, she was still considered an A+ student by her teacher, H. Harrell.

[10] *Modern Man* magazine, September 1956.

Barbara was a cheerleader for her school's football team. During weekends, she and her friends went to the rollerskate rink and visited the Park Movie Theater on the corner of Rockaway Boulevard and 133rd Street, where she dreamed of becoming a star. Rink roller-skating was a very popular recreation among teenagers. Tom Fitzpatrick, who also attended Woodrow Wilson High, recalled, "We had school parties at least once per semester, but usually went weekly to our favorite rinks. We knew which rinks had poles in the middle of the floor, and which ones didn't. There was always a live organist playing the popular songs of the day for us to skate to. There were different numbers such as couples, trios, and free skate. We skated to swing, boogie-woogie, Latin, foxtrot tempos, and novelty numbers."[11]

Every Sunday, Barbara and her parents went to church. Elaine Cox attended the same church and also studied at Woodrow Wilson Vocational High School. "Barbara went to my church, I met her on the bus a lot going home from the subway. She graduated after I did, I graduated January 1946."[12]

At school, Barbara appeared in most of the plays and performed in dance recitals. Acting and dancing are her passions. Just like other girls her age, she loved to model her appearance after stars Betty Grable, Jane Russell, and Lauren Bacall. She was permitted by her parents to take acting lessons at the Brown Adams School. Barbara recalled to columnist Earl Wilson, "I studied acting at the neighborhood playhouse. But I didn't learn anything. The nasty teacher yelled at me. He'd thought I quit. He hated me because I combed my hair and didn't come in like a slob."[13]

A few years later, she told Hedda Hopper, "I worked with Sandy Meisner, and I couldn't stand him and he couldn't stand me. I came to work well-groomed and dressed up, and because of it, he felt I wasn't serious about learning to act. He used to yell at me. That isn't too unusual; you get some directors who feel they have to yell at actors. So, I learned absolutely nothing.

---

[11] Source: email contact with author.
[12] Source: email contact with author.
[13] *The Lima News*, September 30, 1956.

All the things I've learned about acting have come from working with people."[14]

In her graduation year, the one course that raised her interest the most, was cosmetology. Barbara was always proud that she could do her own hair and makeup. As a teenager, she was already very aware of how she presented herself. One of her High School schoolmates, Mike Tierney, received an inscribed photo of Barbara sitting on a fence in a bikini. The bikini was a very daring piece of bathing gear in the 1940s. As a teenager, Barbara clicked better with boys than girls. "I've always had more friends among men than women. I skipped the awkward age and never found it difficult to meet or talk to boys."

Fellow student Tom Fitzpatrick recalled his time at Woodrow Wilson High and an encounter with Barbara. "Barbara was one semester ahead of me, graduating January 1947. She was also one semester ahead of me graduating from Public School 45 January 1943. We were both cheerleaders at Woodrow Wilson Vocational High School. During the mid-1940s, there were disk-hops in the evenings for teens, held at different churches and high school gyms. It was customary for kids to go stag, then meet members of the opposite sex there. Girls would dance together, and a pair of boys would cut in; that's how we would meet. I remember Barbara at such a dance in Richmond Hill High School, where she would dance with a girlfriend, but they would refuse when we boys would ask to cut in. I never knew her to have a boyfriend, and it was said that she went alone to her senior prom and was escorted home by one of the male teacher chaperones. Woodrow Wilson was a vocational school, and I believe Barbara's vocation was 'Beauty Culture', which now would probably be called Cosmetology."[15]

At the insistence of her mother, Barbara entered and won several beauty contests while still at High School. At age seventeen, she was named Miss Loew's Valencia at the old Jamaica movie house. In July 1946, Barbara competed in the Queen of Queens beauty contest. She was selected with five

---

[14] *LA Times*, June 1, 1958.

[15] Source: email contact with author.

other girls to represent Jamaica in the citywide semi-finals of the Miss New York of 1946 contest and received $25 in bonds, makeup kits, and other gifts. The semi-finals were held on August 3 at the Valencia Theatre in Brooklyn. Barbara wasn't selected to proceed to the final on August 26 at Loew's State Theatre in Manhattan. By entering beauty contests, she won several titles. "I was a model, a calendar girl, and a dancer," she recalled in a 1960 interview. "I also was Miss Loew's Paradise, Miss Long Island Duckling, and Miss Loew's Valencia. I never got to be Miss Dill Pickle, though."[16]

Still in school, Barbara was offered a job as a chorus girl with the Copacabana night club, but she turned it down at her parents' request in order to finish her education. Julia encouraged her claim to fame, while George argued with her about the way she presented herself.

To earn extra money while a teenager, Barbara modeled for Gertz department store at 162nd Street and Jamaica Avenue in Downtown Jamaica. Modelling became quite lucrative, and Barbara decided that a name change was appropriate. She shortened Nickerauer to Nichols. Barbara's first regular job after she graduated was in a beauty parlor. With the money she earned at the beauty salon, she paid for her dancing lessons. She disliked her work and focused on a career in showbiz. "I couldn't stand it," she recalled later about her first job, "because I can't stand women. Women don't like me; I don't like them. It's just like in the television plays I do. I just have to talk to a man and his wife thinks right away that I'm making a play for him. And the man generally thinks so, too, for some reason. And all the time, I'm just trying to be polite and friendly. People shouldn't judge a book by the cover, I always say."[17]

One of Barbara's closest girlfriends at the time was Dee Drummond. She was one year older than Barbara and also grew up in Jamaica, Queens. Both girls attended Woodrow Wilson High. Dee was one of the few girls that Barbara was close to in her youth, and the girls became confidants. Dee became the sister Barbara never had.

Drummond's son, Bruce Blau, said, "Dee was definitely an exception

---

[16] *TV guide*, July 23-29, 1960.

[17] *Reading Eagle*, November 21, 1954.

when it came to Barbara's friends. Both only children, both disassociated with their fathers, both number one talents in their High School. Dee has always been a 'guardian of the orphans'-type of person. She helped and mentored many girls that needed friendship and guidance. I remember Barbara looking up to my Mom, she always said to me how much she loved my Mom and how special she was; like a guardian angel. They clicked early on and when Dee saw some of the problems, she was always at the front helping people like Barbara. My Mom drank socially, but always talked about her estranged father being an alcoholic and talked about helping friends like Barbara."[18]

Dee Drummond was born on November 16, 1927, in Vermont, and in her early childhood moved to Kew Gardens, Queens, New York with her mother. There, she met her future friend and roommate, Barbara Nichols. Dee had already been a star soloist in the All-City High School chorus upon graduation in 1944. She studied at the Julliard Institute of Music in New York and started entering beauty and singing contests in her spare time.

Soon after Barbara turned blonde, Dee decided to do the same. Bruce Blau said, "My Mom did not have the level of charisma as Barbara, hence Mom listened to her advice. She was influenced by Barbara, because of not only the closeness; but more significant; their modest upbringings."[19]

Staying close to Barbara, Dee tried following her path into films. After screen-testing for MGM in Los Angeles in 1950, she decided to chase her passion: singing and live stage performing. In 1951, Dee received her first real break in winning the national Judy Garland singing contest. The Music Corporation of America immediately signed her to a contract.

Not wanting to appear as a sex bomb or siren actress, Dee was determined to be a soloist that cherished wearing strapless gowns demurely and sang in the same fashion. From 1956-1966, she performed in all the top New York City clubs, e.g. The Warwick, Copa, El Morocco, Metropole Café, Hotel Roosevelt Grill, and The Latin Quarter. Pairing up with Barbara again in 1960, they did their "Dahling, it's been years!" bit at The Essex House in

[18] Source: email contact with author.
[19] Source: email contact with author.

New York. Dee explained sharing the stage again with Barbara was easy since "... we once starved as roomies." The audience included Rex Harrison and Countess Viviana Crespi, and they were in stitches. In 1961, Barbara and Dee were twisting with each other at the Roundtable night club.

Shunning Hollywood, she still enjoyed being a guest on various TV shows. She became a regular for thirteen weeks on the *Evelyn Tyner Show*. After her appearance on the *Joe Franklin Show*, Dee told everyone that when she performed at Café Bagatelle, Barbara would join her for a "bit of clowning—after all, Barbara and I are used to sharing a room."

Dee tried some film work and landed small extra parts in *The Apartment* (1960), *Butterfield 8* (1960), *Splendor in the Grass* (1961), and *The Manchurian Candidate* (1962). She continued to work in clubs until she remarried in 1968, after which she stayed home for the first time in her life. Dee passed away while residing in Manhattan, New York City on September 14, 2013.

In her youth, Barbara was also close to her cousin, Egbert Carpenter. He was born April 12, 1928. John Carpenter, Egbert's son recalled, "My grandmother on my dad's side, Viola Nickerauer, was married two or three times. Each of the siblings may have been from different dads. She was married to Egbert Dallas Carpenter and after many miscarriages, she supposedly raped my grandfather so she could have another chance at a child which Egbert didn't want to go through any more due to the miscarriages. My dad, Egbert Christopher Carpenter, was born underweight and under size, they called him peanut, they wrapped him in cotton and had him sleep in a cigar box! Viola always spoke and bragged how she seduced my grandfather."

Egbert and Barbara grew up like brother and sister, spending a lot of time together and sharing their dreams of becoming famous. Egbert was a musician, and Barbara wanted to become a great actress. They promised each other that whoever found success first would help the other to success. By the time Barbara became a famous model and worked in several night clubs, she seemed to have forgotten that promise. Around 1954, when Egbert returned from fighting in the Korean war, he hoped Barbara would introduce him to her showbiz connections, but when she didn't, he cut all contact. Egbert was extremely hurt that she seemingly broke all connections with him. He possessed a Dick Haymes-style of voice, and, at that time, was a singer with Johnny Kett and his band. Egbert was offered a recording contract, but when he learned that the Mafia was behind the deal and wanted him to become the toy boy for a big-shot in the organization, he declined the offer.

Carpenter recalled, "My dad was ultra-close to Barbara, and I recall being told by my grandmother that she was afraid they would have sex. She also told me that my dad was very hurt by her bluntly forgetting him when she made it into the big time. My father was a singer, and was her closest confidant. They were out of touch after she got famous due to her never doing anything to help him in the business of entertainment, feeling that he was more talented and would overshadow her. When she began drinking too dad cut off in contact."[20] Egbert Carpenter didn't have any contact with Barbara again for the rest of her life.

Egbert became the director of photography at Metropolitan hospital in Manhattan, a teaching hospital, where he was in charge of public relations photography and taking photos of each surgery operation to show the medical students. He passed away from vascular problems and heart failure on December 30, 2005.

---

[20] Source: email contact with author.

Barbara in front of Woodrow Vocational High, circa 1942.

Barbara sitting on the porch, circa 1943.

Barbara at the roller skating rink, circa 1944.

Barbara - standing in the middle - with boyfriend Henry and fellow High School teenagers, circa 1945. (Courtesy of John Tierney).

Barbara in a bikini, signed for friend Michael Tierney. (Courtesy of John Tierney).

Early pin-up photograph, 1947.

Dee Drummond (Courtesy of Bruce Blau).

Career Girl

EIGHTEEN-YEAR-OLD BARBARA was determined to reach the highest level in show business and went out of her way to reach that goal. Blessed with a strong confidence and healthy self-esteem, she attended casting calls and searched for contacts that could help her climb higher up the ladder of fame—but inside her was the frightened voice of her parents warning their daughter not to overstep the boundaries of good taste.

Just before her nineteenth birthday, Barbara was spotted by actor and Broadway producer Richard Kollmar (1910-1971).[21] He was assembling a

---

[21] Kollmar was married to columnist Dorothy Killgallen between 1940 and 1965. He starred as the title character on the syndicated radio show *Boston Blackie* between 1945 and 1949. He

group of dancers for a song and dance show in South America. Barbara was excited and pled with her parents to let her go. With their eventual consent, Kolmar signed Barbara, Dee, and four other girls to dance in the chorus. The show was to tour the Caribbean. On December 15, 1947 Barbara arranged a Visa for Panama and packed her bags.

The girls appeared in a hotel floor show in the luxurious Hotel Jaragua in Panama City, Panama, between December 17, 1947 and March 6, 1948. Between March 6 and March 30, 1948, Barbara traveled with Kollmar and his troupe to Ciudad Trujillo, Dominican Republic, to appear in several hotel floor-shows over there.[22]

A Panama newspaper mentioned their arrival. "A wonderful group of North American dancers came yesterday from the United States to participate in the big show due next Saturday night for the inauguration of the San Cristobal hotel, just built in Benemerita City. The beautiful dancers will stay in the country for two months and will be presenting their show during this time at the Jaragua hotel. These beautiful women are very famous in all nightclubs of New York: The Copacabana, Latin Quarter, and The Carnival. Their names are: Doris Markey, Gretchen Hauser, Dee Drummond, Frances Wyman, Cece Eames and Barbara Nichols."

Barbara and Dee were the youngest and the least experienced dancers of the troupe. Markey had been a dancer since her childhood, Gretchen Hauser had appeared on Broadway and would go on to dance in movies in the early 1950s. Frances Wyman was a dancer too; she had befriended CeCe Eames when they were in the ensemble of *Toplitzky of Notre Dame* (1946). At the time, CeCe was the most famous of the girls as she had been a dancer in several Broadway musicals since 1939. On January 1, 1945 a *Life* magazine article about calendars placed two paintings of Pin-up artist Earl Moran that featured CeCe. She was also a regular model for Moran and other pin-up artists.

---

was known as a womanizer and is said to have developed a chronic alcohol problem in later years. Kollmar committed suicide in 1971.

[22] Santo Domingo was called Ciudad Trujillo from 1936 to 1961. The dictator, Rafael Trujillo, named the capital after himself.

Kollmar suggested that the reddish-brown-haired Barbara turn blonde, because he didn't have enough blondes for the show. "I became a blonde because my first theatrical job was with a dance troupe that went to South America. The producer said blondes were more successful in South America, and he was right."[23] The men of the Dominican Republic went so wild over the show and the girls that they had to barricade their bedroom door at night to keep them out. High government officials threw several cocktail parties for the American showgirls.

In 1958, Barbara told Hedda Hopper about this trip. "My first job was in the Dominican Republic. I was seventeen and so naïve. There were six girls billed as six sweethearts. We changed acts every two weeks. We were there for two months. We did one show a night under the stars. It was like a vacation. We had a chaperone and everything, which probably was a good thing."

Barbara also recalled meeting Ramfis Trujillo, the eldest son of Dictator Rafael Trujillo, and his mistress, María Martínez, while in South America. "He used to come to see the show with an entourage of bodyguards every night. He used to send me presents. I didn't pay any attention. But one night I did go out with him. He didn't have a bodyguard with him but he had an enormous dog in the car. I said how sweet the dog was and went to pet him and he almost took off my hand! He had a big Lincoln Continental and used to offer me money to go into the casino and gamble. I met his father and he was charming." Calling the harsh dictator a charming man, made Barbara quickly added, "Then I didn't know anything about politics, all I knew was about sitting in the sun and doing one show a night. It's a lovely, lush place. I don't know how it is now but they treated us wonderful; went out of their way to be nice to us."[24]

After her stint in The Dominican Republic, things started happening fast. As soon as Barbara returned to New York, she picked up her modeling work again and appeared in pictorials and on the cover of national publications. At Barbara's request, Cece introduced her to photographer and pin-up artist Earl

---

[23] *Reading Eagle*, November 21, 1954.

[24] Unpublished notes from an interview with Hedda Hopper. Dated 4-10-1958.

Moran. In a mid-1960s magazine interview, Moran—famous for shooting the red velvet nude photos of young Marilyn Monroe—recalled his first meeting with Barbara. "Another rather frightened little blonde lunched one day with Adrian Lopez, the New York magazine editor, and myself. Her name was Barbara Nichols, and apparently her initial fright hasn't stopped her from achieving top starring parts today in films and television."[25]

Gaining more and more self-confidence through modeling, Barbara lost much of her initial fright and let herself be persuaded to pose for more risqué photographs. A 1948 modeling assignment with photographer André de Dienes (1913-1985), who photographed her on the Long Island beach, resulted in an affair with the photographer. Barbara was de Dienes' top model for a while, and the photographs of Barbara running out of the surf and romping around the sand in a black negligee became classics. De Dienes' pictures were quite popular and were featured on various national and international magazine covers.

Not the shy type any longer, Barbara did some nude modeling during the late 1940s for photographers Peter Basch and comedian/photographer Harold Lloyd, among others. She also modelled for renowned artist and illustrator James Montgomery Flagg (1877-1960).[26] Flagg said of Barbara, "She is the one model with absolutely perfect proportions. Most pretty girls have something wrong, but from the top of her head to her little toe Nichols is in perfect condition."[27]

About working as a pin-up model, Barbara said in a 1958 interview, "If you're in cheesecake, as I was, after about a year you've had it. I used to make $20 an hour. For cheesecake, that's good. For fashion modelling, they pay as

---

[25] Lopez (1906-2004) worked as a freelance reporter for The New York American and other newspapers. Mr. Lopez started Laff magazine on his own. He called his publishing house the Volitant Publishing Corporation after a racehorse named Volitant, which turned a $1,000 bet into a $6,000 jackpot.
He soon started a series of detective magazines, and then Sir: A Magazine for Males, a forerunner of later men's magazines. Barbara graced the cover of several of his magazines.

[26] James Montgomery Flagg worked for *Photoplay* magazine and created the world famous poster of 'Uncle Sam.' He created this poster – "I want YOU for U.S. army" – in 1917.

[27] *Sir* magazine, January 1957.

high as $50 an hour. It was alright at the time, but the day came when I was through with the idea."

In between modeling jobs and acting lessons, Barbara danced in chorus lines. She also auditioned and became one of the chorines at the Latin Quarter. Every night, she and the other girls concluded the show with a Cancan dance. The Latin Quarter was based at 1580 Broadway at 47th Street. The Club featured big-name acts, such as Frank Sinatra, Mae West, and Ella Fitzgerald. In the 1940s, striptease star Lili St. Cyr performed her famous bathing beauty routine on the stage of the Latin Quarter. About her time at the Latin Quarter, Barbara recalled later, "Sometimes I was a Cancan girl. And sometimes I just came out and stood around on the stage holding a twig."[28] After a few months Barbara quit the show for two reasons: ". . . the hours and the musicians. Both were too tough to take."[29] After the show, the long-legged showgirl was often asked to sit at the table of customers that were eager to get to know the voluptuous blonde. They feted Barbara with champagne and caviar and invited her to have dinner with them.

While working as a showgirl, Barbara was frequently asked by New York night club owners to become a stripper at their clubs. Although she was flattered and impressed by the salary of $500 per week, Barbara turned them down. She told herself that she was more talented than that and understood that, if once she got a reputation as a stripper, her histrionic talents would be destroyed. "I wanted very much to become a good actress, and I knew I'd never make it once I started peeling."[30]

In 1949, Barbara and her parents moved to 44 Hunters Lane in the city of Huntington on Long Island. Shortly after, Barbara and Dee moved in with fellow models and future movie starlets Carol Ohmart and Gregg Sherwood. They shared an apartment at 145-77 NY Boulevard, Jamaica.

Although she was the youngest, Barbara cast her influence on the other girls, she being influenced by the worldly Sherwood (1923-2011). She had

---

[28] *TV guide*, August 13-19, 1955.

[29] *Cue*, July 23, 1955.

[30] *Chicago Sunday Tribune,* January 17, 1960.

been a model and showgirl for several years and had been married twice before she met Barbara. She had appeared in one movie and made sure she was seen around town dating a famous and especially rich man. In 1953, she married millionaire Horace Dodge Jr. and inherited several million dollars when he passed away in 1963.

In 1949, Barbara signed up with the Bradford Model Agency, which resided at The Dumont Building at 515 Madison Avenue in New York City. There, her statistics were measured at 35-25-35, height 5' 8" (173 cm). For one of her first assignments, twenty-year-old Barbara was featured as one of the models in the first issue of *Cover Girl Models* magazine of November 1949.

Other magazine layouts followed, and on August 16, Barbara and four other semi-finalists were chosen out of thirteen contestants to compete in the Magazine Cover Girl Contest of *See* Magazine. Barbara had appeared on the magazine's July 1948 cover. Donna Lee Hickey, who would later become famous as actress May Wynn, won the seventh round of the contest.

The following week, Barbara was a semi-finalist again, and future actress Jackie Loughery was the winner of that week. May Wynn eventually became Miss *See* of 1951. A newspaper mentions that at the finales, the crowd that cheered the winners numbered at about 5,000. Comedian Joey Adams was the master of ceremonies, and illustrator Russell Patterson headed the board of judges.

Future movie starlet Gloria Pall (1927-2012), working as a model in the New York area herself at the time, recalled a modeling assignment with Barbara, "In the summer of 1949 or 1950, I was hired to go to the White Mountains in New York to a pharmaceutical convention. We were representing 'Tartan Suntan Oil.' We had to leave about 6 a.m. I met the 'boss,' who was going to drive us up there. The other girl was Barbara Nichols. Since she didn't show up, we had to go to her apartment and wake her up and then wait for her to get dressed. Finally, she came out and was very annoyed that we woke her up. She had been out late clubbing the night before and was very grumpy. It was a very long drive in a little Hillman Minx painted up in a tartan plaid sign. I tried to be friendly, and she wouldn't even respond. When we got to our hotel, we were to share a room. We were given bathing suits, shorts, bikinis, and dresses all in tartan plaid prints. Our job was to pose with all the convention members. She wouldn't pose with me in any of the photos. Yet, that was our job. At night, she left our room and disappeared into the night with our 'boss.' He mentioned they played poker all night. She would not utter a solitary word to me the whole trip but was very friendly to him and the conventioneers. It was a long weekend, and each time I tried to talk to her she looked away like I was invisible."[31]

Barbara's modeling work and appearances in magazines soon brought her to the attention of New York's TV producers. Going to casting calls by day, and at night she was the regular date of some big-shot TV producer, hoping by charming those men she will land herself a part in one of their shows.

Gloria Pall also just started out on television, and while making preparations for a TV show, she met Barbara again. "In 1950, I was picking out a costume for *Broadway Open House* starring Jerry Lester and Dagmar. It was the hottest TV show besides Uncle Miltie (Milton Berle). Being the same measurements and height, and was considered a statuesque blond who was good at skits with the comedians, I was used in that capacity as a foil and also as a standby threat to Dagmar in case she got temperamental. So, there I was at the Brooks Costume, owned by actress Geraldine Brooks' family, to be fitted for the next show. In walks Danny or Neil Simon with Barbara for a show she was doing, I believe it was called *Aggie*. Again, I greeted her, and Mr. Simon asked admiringly, 'Who's that?' Again, she ignored my greeting and his question."

The TV show that Gloria mentioned is most likely *Your Show of Shows*. Neil and his brother, Danny Simon, wrote several episodes between 1950 and 1954. Although Barbara did not appear on the show called *Aggie*, she did manage to get Lester to hire her. Barbara played Agathon in Jerry Lester's *Broadway Open House* in March and April 1951. Like Gloria Pall before her, Barbara was supposed to be the stooge in Lester's magician act, "The Great Lester," on each Friday show. Barbara said, "He would pull these tricks that

[31] Source: email contact with author.

never came off and I'd just stand there, feeling kind of silly. Once in a while, I was supposed to throw a pie at him or something."³²

In April 1951, Barbara, not Gloria, posed a permanent threat as a possible replacement for television personality Dagmar on TV's *Broadway Open House*. Comedian Lester was experiencing trouble with the buxom Dagmar. Model and actress Jennie Lewis was hired to play Dagmar as a real dumb blonde. She did this very effectively and turned out to be a comedienne with razor sharp wit. Soon, Dagmar was easily the most popular cast member on the show.

Lester resented being upstaged by Dagmar and tried to undermine her success by hiring Barbara, but Dagmar's popularity kept growing. At the height of her popularity, she received around 8,000 fan letters a month. Through her agent, Danny Hollywood, she stated that Lester wasn't treating her right and had not given her the right kind of material to work with. She threatened not to sign her contract, to which Lester gave her a deadline: she had to sign and renew her contract by expiration time May 25, 1951, or else Barbara would take her spot on the show. Lester even tried to get the network so far as to sack Dagmar, but NBC officials refused.

Barbara, hoping to become just as popular as Dagmar, added fuel to the fire by saying that she was a different type physically than Dagmar, and that she didn't need a paper to read from. Barbara also commented on the feud between her and Dagmar. "We say hello, but that's all. We don't talk, otherwise. But don't blame me. I'm a conversationalist, by nature."³³ Eventually, Lester walked off his own show in May 1951, and Dagmar carried on as host. On July 16, 1951, she was featured on the front cover of *Life* magazine. The TV show came to an end one month later.

Lester, already negotiating a new show, asked Barbara to stay out of television until he had signed the new deal. He told Barbara that he wanted her to be on his show when he returned in the fall. He didn't want her to be identified with any other program. When Lester joined Bob Hope and

---

³² *TV guide*, August 13-19, 1955.
³³ *Sunday Herald*, April 22, 1951.

Fred Allen as one of the rotating stars of *Sound Off Time*, Barbara was there with him, but Lester wouldn't allow himself to be upstaged by another sharp comedienne.

Barbara was so effective in her performances that she was liked by the public and noted by the press as a new discovery to take notice of. "At this, editors around the country sat up and took real notice of the impressively pretty blonde with the breath taking figure, kittenish eyes, delightful smile and little girl voice. Writers and photographers were dispatched to do features on her."[34]

Not liking what was happening Lester went into action. "The moment it was apparent that a vast publicity harvest was about to come Agathon's way she was, intimates say, finished on the Lester show."[35]

Esquire magazine had featured Barbara as their Pin-up Model of the Month several times in 1951. She had posed for pin-up artist Al Moore a year earlier and worked for him about three years in total, starting in 1948. Moore called her one of his favorite models because he thought Barbara had "an enormous appeal for men. In addition, she's pleasant and easy to work with."[36] In 1951, Moore sent Barbara a Christmas card to thank her again for making the calendar such a success.[37]

Because of Moore's calendar, her appearances on TV, and her reputation as a regular partygoer in the New York nightlife, Barbara was noticed by producer Jule Styne and was chosen to audition for a part in his upcoming Broadway production of *Pal Joey*. Barbara landed the small part of Valerie, a hair-brained striptease/showgirl. About the auditions, Barbara recalled, "I didn't know I was funny until Richard Rodgers hired me to play a stripper in the 1952 revival of *Pal Joey*. I guess I must have been funny when I read for

---

[34] *New England TV Guide*, Week of December 7, 1951.

[35] *New England TV Guide*, Week of December 7, 1951.

[36] *True – The Man's Magazine*, June, 1951.

[37] The card read: "Dear Barbara, Besides best wishes for the holiday season, this note is to express thanks for your help in making the 1951 Esquire calendar a succes. As I recall you posed for the Jan., March, April, August and Nov. pages in the 1951 Calendar and several in the 1950. Thanks again, Al Moore."

Rodgers. He fell down laughing."[38] Rodgers was the Music Composer of the play, he wrote the show's music and lyrics together with Lorenz Hart.

Originally, it was a one-line part, but presumably Barbara said her line, "Can I recite now?" so well that director David Alexander took all the other chorus girls' lines away and used them to build up a little part for Barbara. Barbara assured Philip Minoff, reporter for *Cue* magazine, that her colleagues didn't blame her for the loss of their lines.

Barbara remembered, "Oh, they were really swell about it. You see, I'm a hard girl to get mad at. I'm not ambitious and I'm not a driver. And I like doing things for people. In the *Pal Joey* company, I used to do the girls' hair for them all the time. That's the kind of person I am."[39]

In retrospect, it seems more likely that Barbara wasn't telling the reporter that she was more like the kind of aspiring actress that would do just that little extra to get the director or producer so far as to put her in the spotlight over the other showgirls.

---

[38] *TV Guide*, July 23-29, 1960.
[39] *Cue*, July 23, 1955.

Barbara with roommates Gregg Sherwood and Carol Ohmart posing for a magazine shoot in December 1947.

Gregg Sherwood, Carol Ohmart, and Barbara, December 1947.

Barbara at the pool in the Domenican Republic, 1948.

Beauty Pageant contestant, 1948.

Barbara modeling for an article in a Detective magazine, 1948. (Courtesy of Janice Pease).

Modeling, 1948. (Courtesy of Janice Pease)

Barbara at the beach, 1949 (Courtesy of Janice Pease).

Barbara with an unknown suitor, 1950.

Calendar sheet with Barbara, from Esquire Magazine, 1950.

Modeling photo, 1950. (Courtesy of Janice Pease).

Modeling photo, 1950.

Barbara gives a sultry look, 1950.

Pinup photo, 1951.

Barbara in a daring pose, 1951. (Courtesy of Janice Pease).

Barbara with a (boy)friend under the boardwalk, 1951.

Breakthrough

IN DECEMBER 1951, columnist Earl Wilson listed vocalist Kathy Barr, Marilyn Monroe, and Barbara as the year's outstanding figures. The next year, he hired Barbara to appear as his "secretary" on his TV column called *Stage Entrance*. "I had a TV show a long time back," he recalled, "and we hired her to play the part of Taffy Tuttle, my lame-brained secretary. Barbara's got a good-looking face and a fine body, and she's a nice girl. One day she showed up in an outfit with an unusually low neck. The producer and director had approved the outfit, so we went on the air without any reservations. But some of the brass caught the show and raised the roof. They said, 'Never let that girl on the show again.' It was too bad because it wasn't Barbara's fault at all."[40]

---

[40] *Modern Man*, December 1956.

Barbara commented about the incident a couple of years later. "They were always worrying about me, especially, I've worn dresses that were high in front, and they still add a piece of material. Anyway, the dress doesn't matter. You can show a lot in your face, in your eyes, in your attitude. If I play a sexy part, I walk sexy and think sexy."

Meanwhile, Barbara visited the burlesque bars and strip joints at 52nd street to watch the exotic dancers perform in preparation for her part as a burlesque showgirl in *Pal Joey*. Opening January 3, 1952 at the Broadhurst Theatre, *Pal Joey* ran for a total of 540 performances. The show closed on Broadway on April 18, 1953. Set in Chicago in the late 1930s, it shows Joey Evans, a manipulative small-time nightclub performer, whose ambitions lead him into an affair with the wealthy, middle-aged and married Vera Simpson and a showgirl named Linda English at the same time. Actor Harold Lang played Joey, Pat Northrop played Linda English, and Vivienne Segal was seen in the role of Vera Simpson.[41]

The show was a smash and a sell-out. Audiences came in droves, on a Broadway that already had *The King and I*, *Guys and Dolls*, and *South Pacific* playing in the other theatres. *Sir!* magazine wrote in a pictorial on Barbara, "When *Pal Joey* was revived on Broadway, it owed much of its revival success to the talented, ambitious cast. Barbara Nichols is typical of the young and talented group which made the play an outstanding Broadway hit. Barbara Nichols takes the part of a sexy but dumb girlfriend. Barbara gives the part a corking performance despite the fact that she has only fifteen lines of dialogue."[42]

On July 12, Barbara and her parents attended the wedding of her cousin, Eileen Wurst-Harmann, in Great Neck. In September 1952, Barbara was operated on to get her nose bobbed. A little lump on her nose was removed, and within a month, she was back on the stage. When the show closed in New York City, Barbara and the *Pal Joey* cast traveled to Washington in April,

---

[41] In the movie of 1957, Barbara played Gladys Bumps, a chorus girl who takes an instant dislike to Joey. The role was played by Helen Gallagher in the 1952 play.

[42] November 1952.

performed at the Shubert Theatre in Chicago in May and June, and arrived in San Francisco in September, 1953.

Because of the show, Barbara became sort of a celebrity of her own. She was featured in a couple of pin-up magazines and caught the eye of a famous TV actor. She dated TV's Superman, George Reeves (1914-1959), for a while, but then was warned to back off. John Cohan, a Hollywood psychic, who counted Barbara among his clients, remembered, "Barbara went out with George Reeves for a while but she was terrified of his girlfriend of many years, Toni Mannix. Toni was still married to her husband a big Studio Maven. He approved of her affair with George Reeves because he couldn't perform as a husband in the bedroom. Barbara feared Toni would have her beaten up, so she did stop the dating with George."[43]

Toni Mannix, a former actress and dancer in the 1920s, was known as an outspoken lady with ties to the mob. Eddie Mannix is best remembered for his protective work of the Hollywood stars and work as a "fixer," in which he was able to hide aspects of their colorful private lives to keep their clean screen image.[44] Due to her marriage with the studio executive, Toni knew secrets to blackmail stars with, and for that reason, was an influential and feared woman in Hollywood of the 1940s and 1950s.

For the program booklet of *Pal Joey*, Barbara was sent to photographer Peter Basch to shoot her publicity photos. Many of these photos were used to grace the covers of national magazines *Art Photography* and *Laff*. Peter Basch described in 1955 what made a good pin-up model for him. "The most decisive element in any cheesecake photograph is the model. She, and she alone decides the success or failure of a single picture or a picture set. It is not enough for the model to be attractive physically. In many instances her personality far outweighs her feature value. Many top models in this category are not truly beautiful women. Even some, who have risen to stardom in fields other than magazine photography, have done so on the strength of their tremendous sex appeal rather than because of their face or figure. The girl who

---

[43] Source: email contact with author.
[44] *The Telegraph*, February 1, 2015.

possesses the necessary ingredients is an invaluable aid to the man behind the camera. If she is a professional, her past experience has taught her to use—and often, in the case of Pat Hall and Barbara Nichols to name but two pros—to provide eye-catching costumes, as well as an uncanny knack for posing provocatively."[45]

Basch worked with Barbara on many other assignments. He admired her ability to act while posing and was enthusiastic about her ability to convey humor in a cheesecake photograph.

In March 1953, Barbara was named "Miss Welder" by the National Eutectic Welders' Clubs. She was selected as "the girl we would like most to weld with." This dubious title was previously given to actress Denise Darcel. (Barbara's later successor was no one less than Italian actress Sophia Loren.)

In Chicago, Barbara met producer Stanley Rubin (1917-2014), who fell in love with her and—according to the press—wooed her with crates of oranges, sides of beef, and other practical gifts. The lovers spent a lot of time together when *Pal Joey* had its summer stop in July and August, but they were separated after that summer.

In September, Barbara left to work in San Francisco. She had a new friend to accompany her to rehearsals and performances—a black poodle named Samson, a gift from Sam Houston III, one of her admirers. After the San Francisco run of *Pal Joey*, Barbara left the cast and was replaced by starlet Mabel Rea.[46]

In May 1953, Stanley Rubin was producing *River of No Return* (1954), a movie with Marilyn Monroe. Rubin secured a small part for Barbara. Interior shooting at the 20th Century Fox sound stages was done in June and July, the first time she worked in a Hollywood movie production. Although her part as a saloon girl was small, working on a movie set was an experience she hoped to repeat soon.

---

[45] *Peter Basch's Glamour Photography*, 1956.

[46] Mabel Rea (1932-1968) also played a small part in the film version of Pal Joey (1957). The 36-year-old Miss Rea, a onetime Rockette, was killed when the car in which she was riding slammed into a utility pole.

Following her film debut, Barbara filmed an episode of TV's *Studio One* titled "Confessions of a Nervous Man," which aired on November 30, 1953. Introduced by playwright George Axelrod, the story is about a writer played by Art Carney, who is anxiously awaiting the reviews for his new play, *The Seven Year Itch*. The story takes place at a nightclub. Barbara is one of the guests that discuss the play and Axelrod's success. While sipping a glass of Champagne, she discusses the title of the play: "I adored this play, but *The Seven Year Itch* . . . what a repulsive title. I begged George to change it." There are a couple more scenes in which Barbara is seen and heard in this 50-minute teleplay. Paul Nickell, the director of the show, later commented, "Although this was not one of the most popular shows we have done, it was great fun for those who put it on." George Axelrod wrote the script as a big spoof for those "in the know" in television. Axelrod later approached Barbara to play Rita Marlowe in his newest stage play, *Will Success Spoil Rock Hunter?*, which was a spoof on Hollywood.

No further film work in Hollywood commenced after Barbara's movie debut. However, TV work was aplenty. Barbara was always cast as a blonde femme fatale, a girl who comes between two lovers and almost breaks up their romance. Barbara commented, "Sometimes I would like to play the other girl's part. The nice, sweet young thing who wins the boy at the end of the play, overcoming all obstacles, including the main one, the girl who tries to lure the hero away from his sweetheart. That's me." She added, "I am typed, so I guess there is nothing I can do about it. Of course, it's a good thing to be typed, because when a part comes along for a girl who is a menace, right away the producers and directors think of me. I've had writers tell me that when they wrote a play for television they would have me in mind when they wrote it."[47]

In May, Columbia studios hired Barbara as the stand-in for actress Judy Holliday in the movie *Phffft* (1954). During the production, Judy suffered from a viral infection. She was under pretty heavy sedation most of the time. In fact, after a scene was shot, she tottered off to bed and stayed there, limp

---

[47] *Reading Eagle*, November 21, 1954.

and ill, until time for the next one. Barbara stood in for Holliday in most of the movie's long shots.

Stanley Rubin couldn't fix Barbara up with another job, and when she returned to New York on April 6, 1954 after visiting Rubin in Hollywood, she knew the affair was over. On July 25, Rubin married actress Kathleen Hughes. George B. Druxman, a friend of Rubin recalled that Rubin told him he was rather disappointed with the way Barbara behaved when she had a drink too many. In Rubin's opinion, she had a drinking problem.[48]

Kathleen Hughes remembered that Barbara and her husband stayed on friendly terms once she'd married Rubin. Hughes. "All I know about her is that my husband used to date her before we got married. She came to our house at least once. She came to one of our parties. I could not say that I knew her very well."[49]

During December 1954 and January 1955, Barbara and comedian Jack Carter were reported as a regular two-some in the Manhattan nightlife. Actress Paula Stewart, who would become Carter's wife in 1961, and became Barbara's friend when they appeared in the stage musical, *Let It Ride!* (1961), claims the Carter-Nichols connection seems hardly likely. "As far as I knew, Jack never was a 'couple' with Barbara. She didn't particularly like him. She came to visit us frequently. No hanky panky then. She thought he was funny but brash. He inferred to the press that she was 'the mother of my child' [Jack and Paula's son was born in 1966], a totally nasty thing to say!"[50] Carter and Stewart were divorced in 1970. Carter later told Stewart he never had anything to do with Barbara. Carter claimed that Barbara was always hanging around celebrities to make it seem like she was with them.

During winter 1954, Barbara rehearsed for a new stage play to be presented in Palm Beach, Florida. In the play called *Firecrackers*, actor Steve Cochran (1917-1965) played the part of Bart Ashley, a young bachelor of

---

[48] Source: email contact with author.

[49] Source: telephone conversation with author, 7-14-2014.

[50] Source: email contact with author.

the publishing field, who is chased by four young women. Mary Evelyn Ducey, Priscilla Gillette, and Diana Douglas played three of the girls. Barbara played the fourth, Eloise Purcell, a nightclub entertainer with a "Champagne Complex." In the play, there was a clever dance sequence in which Barbara thrust a delightful jolt in Bart's direction. Ashley's normal week of a date-a-night with a different girl was upset, because all the girls decided to marry him. What followed was almost two full hours of hilarious situations and sparkling dialogue until Ashley's problems were solved to his complete satisfaction.

The Palm Beach Post reviewed playwright Leonard Kantor's comedy *Firecrackers*, which had its premiere at the Palm Beach Playhouse on February 21, 1955. The review read in part: "*Firecrackers* is a theatrical invention of sophisticated wit and humor, with a cast of attractive and capable actors and actresses who spin the play along like a top . . . 'Blondie' (Eloise) who wriggles and giggles, loses miserably in the chase when she changes her tune from one of sheer physical appeal to become a conversationalist."

The play was Broadway bound later that spring or early fall under the direction of Paul Crabtree, but it never reached New York. After the run in Palm Beach, the show closed.

During rehearsals, Barbara fell in love with Steve Cochran. He was known as a wild guy. Just like his character in the play, he loved women, he loved to party, and he drank heavily. Barbara was attracted to his wild image and soon they were engaged in a hot affair. Their idyll lasted one winter.

Back in New York in March, Barbara's new hairdo caused her to be mistaken for Marilyn Monroe when she visited the nightclub, El Morocco. As a result, she received the tag "Brooklyn's Marilyn Monroe." Wanting to be an original, she soon dyed her hair in a dark brown color.

In May 1955, Barbara traveled to the West Indies to start filming a movie called *Manfish*. Unlike her movie debut the year before, *Manfish* was entirely filmed on location on the island of Jamaica. William Lee Wilder directed the movie, and John Bromfield and Lon Chaney Jr. were cast for the leading parts. The story revolves around a sailor, who discovers a skeleton at the bottom of the sea holding a bottle. He retrieves a ring and a map from it. He then tries to force a man with a matching ring to produce his half of the map so he can go treasure hunting.

Barbara, tanned and with her new dark brown hair, is almost unrecognizable as Mimi, a singer/entertainer and girlfriend of John Bromfield. She translates the map, which is written in French, for Bromfield. She has a couple of other scenes and sings one song, "Beware of the Caribbean," which is also the theme song that is heard when the end titles roll. British *Picturegoer* magazine gave the movie a "fair" rating. About Barbara, they wrote, "The girls—Barbara Nichols and Tessa Prendergast—know how to use their curves to advantage, though."

Barbara in costume for the stage musical *Pal Joey*, 1952.

Pal Joey stage number, 1952.

Barbara as Miss Welder of 1953. (Courtesy of Janice Pease).

Barbara working in a tv-show in 1953. (Courtesy of Janice Pease).

Barbara and Harpo Marx, 1953. (Courtesy of Janice Pease).

Barbara and Samson. (Courtesy of Janice Pease).

Barbara and unknown man, 1953.

Magazine clipping with Barbara and Steve Cochran.

Barbara with Richard Egan and unknown lady, 1954.

Barbara and Jack Carter, 1955.

Barbara in Jamaica, filming *Manfish*, 1955. (Courtesy of Janice Pease).

Manfish lobbycard (1956).

Movie Star

When Barbara returned to Hollywood from Jamaica in June, she met up with Steve Cochran again and they renewed their romance. While Barbara was filming on Jamaica and away in New York, Cochran was seen around town with Warner Bros. starlet Jayne Mansfield. Cochran had been under contract to Warner Bros. from 1949 until 1952, and the studio shaped Barbara's early movie career and professional personality.

Jack Warner, the youngest of twelve children of Jewish immigrants, was the studio boss and ruled his studio with an iron fist. Together with three of his brothers, he founded the studio in 1923. In the 1930s and 1940s, the studio had James Cagney, Edward G. Robinson, Humphrey Bogart, Errol Flynn, Bette Davis, and Joan Crawford under contract. Gangster movies, adventure films, and social dramas were their forte. In the 1950s, clean cut Doris Day was Warner Bros.' main attraction, and wholesome, family-oriented movies were the studio's main output.

In spring 1955, Warner Bros. signed Barbara for a movie to be filmed on location in New York City. In the Canadian TV broadcast of *Tabloid*, she explains how she got the part: "I played a sexy maid, called Rosalie, on the Sid Caesar Show, and Warner Bros. saw it and signed me for *Miracle in the Rain*. They felt I was right for the part," which, according to Barbara, had nothing to do with the way she looked. In the TV interview, Barbara stresses that her acting ability turned the scale.[51]

Miracle in the Rain was filmed between mid-May and July 9, 1955. The film tells the story of a secretary, played by Jane Wyman, who falls in love with a G.I., Van Johnson, who is sent to war and killed. Barbara played the newlywed, Arlene Parker, née Witchy. Pin-up girl Arlene is also an exotic dancer and singer, who made a name for herself as "the kiss-less bride" when she divorced her first husband, a millionaire from Long Island. "She made one lousy mistake, she forgot to ask for a settlement. She could have shook him down for a million," husband Alan King tells Johnson.

Barbara, in a blonde wig, is featured in two scenes. In the first, she's in Central Park, posing for the pictures her husband is making of her. The newlyweds make the acquaintance of Johnson and Wyman. Wyman later accompanies King to Barbara's performance, singing "With Plenty of Money and You." Barbara's own interpretation of Arlene's act was considered too hot by the film's producers, so they hired a dance teacher to teach her the new moves. "I couldn't dance the way I wanted to," she later told. "I got too crazy for them. If you read between the curves, honey, they're there because it's the mental-est striptease you ever saw."[52]

Barbara recalled the shooting of her first scene in the movie. "In the

[51] *Tabloid*, July 3, 1957.
[52] June 24, 1955.

scene, I was supposed to meet Van Johnson the first day I was married to another man. As my husband and I walked through the park, we met Van and I emoted. The director yelled, 'Cut! 'Barbara,' he said 'a new bride is not supposed to be that friendly with another man.' I said, 'I couldn't help it. Van's just too darn cute.'"[53]

The New York Times wrote that it found the movie to be too melodramatic. The newspaper mentioned Barbara in the film's review: ". . . Alan King, as a Brooklynese soldier, and Barbara Nichols, his brassy, blonde, simple, stripteaser bride, adds a helpful bit of comedy."

In between filming *Miracle in the Rain,* Barbara was chosen by comedian Sid Caesar to be his summer TV replacement with comedian Phil Foster and singer Bill Hayes. Barbara had worked with Caesar earlier on *Your Show of Shows* in 1951 and *Caesar's Hour* two years after that. Caesar's shows reached as many as 60 million viewers weekly.

Caesar wanted Barbara to play Foster's wife on *Caesar's Presents.* It was a big part, and one of the writers, worried about Barbara's lack of experience, pointed out she'd fluffed lines on many shows. Barbara handled that expertly. "That's because I've always been miscast as a dumb blonde, but I'm not dumb," she explained. Turning to Caesar, she said, "I know I'll make a good married woman." Caesar hired her on the spot.

The chemistry between Foster and Barbara was unsuccessful, and before she knew it, she was written off the show. No reason was ever given, but a cast member analysed it this way: "It may sound silly, but the reason she was dropped wasn't her inability to handle lines. Her looks and figure and come-hither expression made her with the public. What probably happened was that the boys who put the show together learned too early that the come-hither expression was only a smokescreen for the real go-away, what-are-you-doing personality the kid's definitely got."[54]

Barbara stated to the press, "I wasn't happy with Phil and he wasn't happy with me. I quit. I went out to Hollywood to do a stage show, called *Joy Ride,*

---

[53] *Oakland Tribune,* March 4, 1956.

[54] *Confidential Flash,* June 17, 1961.

and everything happened, crazy!" Adding, "I've always had good timing. I worked with Sid Caesar and Red Buttons in the day when they used to give newcomers a chance on TV. Then, I did summer stock and *Pal Joey* on Broadway, so by the time I started to do movies I felt pretty secure."

All this time, Barbara had kept in touch with Steve Cochran. She visited him in July while he was filming *Come Next Spring* (1956) on location in Sacramento, California. Apart from Cochran, Barbara also dated actor Hal March in August and September of 1955. In the newspapers, her name was often linked to many famous men. Barbara once said about this, "You know I read my name in the papers linked with people I've hardly met, going to this restaurant or that. It must be the publicity people for the restaurants; they make up people when they don't find them there."

Cochran left Hollywood in November 1955 to travel to Great Britain, where he appeared in *The Weapon* (1956) with Lizabeth Scott. He also had fun with buxom blonde Sabrina after work.

A month later in December, Barbara left for Los Angeles to rehearse for the musical revue, *Joy Ride,* and to take part in *The Wild Party* (1956) with Anthony Quinn. Former roommate Carol Ohmart has a large part in the movie, but shares no scenes with Barbara. The movie is a raw melodrama with sexual overtones that was considered hot stuff back in 1956. *The Wild Party* was filmed between January 26 and March. Barbara plays the small part of the showgirl girlfriend of Paul Stewart, and is seen in one scene only.

Joy Ride opened in January 1956 at the Huntington Hartford Theatre in Los Angeles and closed in June 1956 at the Shubert Theatre in Chicago, failing to arrive in New York for a Broadway opening. Conrad Janis, Aileen Stanley Jr., and Dorothy Greener starred, while Barbara once more played a burlesque queen. "In my opening scene," she said, "I'm dropped from the ceiling on a rope wearing only letters for a costume. They spell out 'Man's Inhumanity to Man.'" Barbara hated to ride the swing high above the stage every time she had to go on. She told columnist Sidney Skolsky, "I got dizzy and frightened and I was always afraid one of the stagehands would let go of the rope or something awful like that." Luckily, no accidents occurred.

A review read in part, "Barbara Nichols nearly stole the show with her song, "Please Mr. Glover, Don't Discover Me" at last night's opening...."[55]

Actor and jazz trombone player Conrad Janis (1928) had met Barbara earlier when they appeared together in the TV show *Danger*'s episode "Sandy River Blues" that aired on April 12, 1955. Janis remembered that Barbara was pleasant to everyone working on *Joy Ride*. "My memories of *Joy Ride* are mixed," he said, "Just after I accepted, I was given the opportunity to star in several movies originally given to James Dean just before he sadly died. But the producer of *Joy Ride*, Huntington Hartford, though he released many of the other actors, wouldn't release my contract to allow me one of the greatest opportunities of my life at the time. It was a devastating loss to me, and so many of the other actors benefited from being released. It's just one of the strange laws of our industry. I therefore don't have the same impressions of the play as others might."[56]

Barbara was inevitably being compared with Marilyn Monroe and Jayne Mansfield. When producers were casting for a sexy blonde to play Jayne Mansfield's role in the West Coast company of *Will Success Spoil Rock Hunter?*, Barbara turned them down flat. She didn't want to be another Jayne Mansfield doing another Marilyn Monroe. About the rivalry between Jayne and Marilyn, she later commented, "Let them go their way and I'll go mine. There's plenty of money and glory for all of us without climbing on each other to reach the top of the heap."[57]

For the "Glamour Doll" episode of the TV series *It's a Great Life*, Barbara was cast to play a glamorous actress called Caroline Cabot, and her dialogue revealed that the writers were hinting at Marilyn Monroe. Tommy Noonan, a great fan of Cabot, confesses to her that he watched her movie, *Bathing Beauty*, three times. "You look great in a bathing suit." To which, Caroline answers: "I'm not gonna wear them anymore. I'm gonna do different kind of pictures. Pictures that make people think," referring to the statement

---

[55] *Mirror News*, January 13, 1956.

[56] Source: email contact with author.

[57] *Modern Man* magazine, September 1956.

Monroe had made to leave Hollywood for New York to take acting lessons at The Actor's Studio. To further emphasize the Monroe character, Barbara is wearing a dress Monroe had worn in *How to Marry a Millionaire*, in the next scene.

Joy Ride proved to be Barbara's ticket to Hollywood fame. Many producers offered her a part in their upcoming productions. She was announced to play a gangster's moll with showbiz aspirations in 20th Century Fox production *The Best Things in Life are Free* (1956). However, that part was played by Roxanne Arlen, who provided a delightful "Barbara Nichols" imitation as the talentless singer Perky Nichols.

Instead, Barbara signed a contract at Warner Bros. for the film version of the stage musical, *The Pajama Game* (1957). A couple of years earlier, she had been offered the same role in the Broadway play, but her agent nixed it because of the low salary. Barbara commented, "If I'd done the play, I probably wouldn't be in the movie now. They'd say I wasn't the type."

In June, she was scheduled to start working on *The King and Four Queens* (1956), with Clark Gable and Eleanor Parker.

Director Fritz Lang wanted to haul her out of *Joy Ride* to play a leading role in his next movie, *Beyond a Reasonable Doubt*, but the producers of the show, Huntington Hartford and Ray Golden, would not let her go. Eventually, they reached an agreement, and in March, Barbara signed a contract with producer Bert E. Friedlob. He was a womanizer, and while working on the movie, the press mentioned that Barbara was having an affair with him, only to report one month later, that "Trudy Wroe, not Barbara Nichols, is the only doll in producer Bert Friedlob's life."

Friedlob died of cancer several months after the release of *Beyond a Reasonable*. Working with producer Friedlob wasn't a pleasant experience for anyone involved. Fritz Lang and Friedlob fought about everything. Friedlob forced Dana Andrews on Lang. Andrews, who was drinking throughout the filming, added to Lang's despair.⁵⁸ When the movie was finished, director Lang left Hollywood and returned to Europe.

In *Beyond a Reasonable Doubt,* Barbara plays Burlesque Stripper Dolly Moore. Barbara commented about her Burlesque act, "I hope I see it before it's all cut out!" Just like she did a few years ago in preparation for her part in *Pal Joey,* she began by reviewing girls at Los Angeles nightclubs and striptease joints to see if anything had been added since she last witnessed a performance. "Watching them dames made me feel as bored as they looked. I felt like climbing on the stage, tearing of my clothes and showing them that sex should be passion and sin. A stripper has to fry the guys six rows in the back. She has to make his hormones percolate."⁵⁹ For two long months, Barbara woke at six a.m., worked at RKO studios during the day, and worked on the stage until midnight. The production was completed on August 7, 1956.

The story of *Beyond a Reasonable Doubt* involves a reporter, Dana Andrews, who has himself framed for the murder of a stripper in order to expose the incompetence of the police and the fallacy of capital punishment. Fifteen minutes into the movie, Barbara and Robin Raymond make their first appearance, when they're being questioned by the police about their murdered colleague. A few minutes later, we see Barbara as Dolly performing a striptease in the Burlesque House.

After the show, Dana Andrews seeks contact with her at the Diner across the street. He accidentally spills his drink over her dress. Andrews asks Dolly if he can get in touch with her to take care of the costs of dry-cleaning. "You touched enough already," Dolly replies.

The next day Andrews visits Dolly in her dressing room. He pays $100 for the dry cleaning costs and immediately Dolly's attitude towards him changes. She purrs, "I'm sorry I lost my temper, but my performances are very tiring." Warned by Robin Raymond about what happened to their murdered

---

⁵⁸ Andrews (1909-1992) took steps to curb his addiction and in his later years was an outspoken member of the National Council on Alcoholism who decried public refusal to face the problem.

⁵⁹ *Modern Man* magazine, September 1956.

colleague, Dolly decides to call the police station. The police follow the couple on their date the next evening. Andrews notices that he's being followed and, as part of his plan, forces Dolly to kiss him. When she screams out, the police come to her rescue and bring Andrews to the police station. Andrews is held as a suspect and Dolly is one of the witnesses in the court scenes. It's the last scene Barbara was seen in.

In the last twenty minutes of the movie, more evidence against Andrews is built up, and at the end, he is found guilty of murdering Dolly's colleague.

Co-star Robin Raymond was enthusiastic about working with Barbara, "This girl talks dialogue. She's completely uninhibited in what she says. The first day I went to lunch with her, waitresses fainted dead away over dropped bowls of chili."

Barbara loved the part she got to play. "She's a crazy doll, man, with crazy lines and clothes. Man, it's a personality seller."[60] Personality was what Barbara wanted to sell as a celebrity.

She openly criticized Marilyn Monroe, and sex siren actresses like her, for wanting to act. Barbara told the press, "I'll never follow Marilyn's wiggles into the 'I-want-to-be-a-great-actress' league. It's personality that sells in the movies, not great acting. I've listened to people who told me I should go to dramatic school, but that's all I do, just listen. Personality is what I'm dishing up. I'm going to be myself, not something produced by a dramatic school. I don't think I'm any great actress. I think maybe I'm a personality. You know how Gary Cooper is always playing Gary Cooper? Well, I'm very happy just being Barbara Nichols most of the time."

---

[60] *Corpus Christi Times*, April 13, 1956.

Warner Bros. publicity photo.

Barbara in *Miracle in the Rain* with Alan King and Van Johnson, 1956.

Miracle in the Rain, 1956.

Barbara in a publicity photo for *Miracle in the Rain*, 1956.

The Wild Party, 1956.

Publicity photo for *Joyride*, 1956.

Barbara in a publicity photo for *Beyond a Reasonable Doubt*, 1956.

Barbara with Edward Binns and Robin Raymond in *Beyond a Reasonable Doubt*, 1956.

Beyond a Reasonable Doubt, 1956.

Barbara in a publicity photo for *Beyond a Reasonable Doubt*, 1956.

Barbara in *Beyond a Reasonable Doubt* with Dana Andrews, 1956.

The King and the Girl from Queens

BARBARA'S NEXT FILM PROJECT got her all excited. "I called my mother to tell her I was in a picture with Clark Gable. She says, 'but are you going with anybody?' She'd be so happy when I got married and settled down."[61] Barbara was ecstatic about working with "The King of Hollywood" and had nothing but praise for him. "To me, he is what a movie star should be and so often isn't. I think any woman who meets him even once could never forget the meeting. I will always remember the things he has said to me."

In April 1956, Clark had interviewed and selected Barbara personally,

---

[61] *The Lima News*, September 30, 1956.

after seeing her performance in the rushes of *Beyond a Reasonable Doubt*. He liked her spirit. Barbara, Sara Shane, and Jean Willes were chosen from seventeen other actresses tested for the part of Jo Van Fleet's daughters-in-law.

Glamour photographer Bernard of Hollywood had introduced Gable and Barbara to each other a couple of years earlier. "I introduced Joi Lansing and Barbara to Clark Gable. We ordered exotic dishes at Don the Beachcomber's. Clark played it cool that night. Three years later, Barbara landed a part in his production *The King and Four Queens*."[62]

Photoplay magazine dedicated an article to Barbara's affection for Gable and also described that Barbara befriended Gable's wife Kay while filming. The article mentioned Barbara's casting by Gable and read in part, "'How old are you?' he had asked at their first meeting in the studio office. 'How old do you want me to be?' Barbara had replied, and everybody laughed, Clark the hardest of all. 'I was off the ice then,' Barbara said.

"She kept thinking, 'How sweet he is,' knowing it was a word he would not like, but the only one she could think of to describe him. She didn't know then the kind of part for which she was being considered or how old she was supposed to be. She just kept hoping she was the right age and the right type, because by that time she wanted that part more than she had ever wanted anything else."

Clark began to explain the kind of girl Barbara would play in *The King and Four Queens*. "'He made her so real to me,'" Barbara recalled, "'that I began to feel like that girl. He asked what other things I had done. I told him about the role of the burlesque dancer in *Miracle in the Rain*, and my bigger and more recent part in *Beyond a Reasonable Doubt*, with Dana Andrews and Joan Fontaine. Mr. Gable listened attentively. Then he asked if I would mind making a test with him. Would I mind?'"[63]

Gable was giving Barbara all the breaks in their scenes together. He coached her on where to look, showed her where her key light was. "I had

---

[62] Bernard, Susan. *Bernard of Hollywood – The Ultimate Pin-up Book*. Cologne: Taschen, 2002.

[63] *Photoplay* magazine, February 1957.

done a great deal of television in New York, and had learned to appreciate helpful friendliness from most fellow actors and directors, but I really didn't expect that kind of help from a star like Mr. Gable. When one particular scene in the film bothered me, he took me aside and discussed the scene and rehearsed all the lines with me. It was a difficult bit, in which little nuances, conveyed in only a few words and gestures, were all-important."[64]

Clark Gable was known as a practical joker. As such, he had a wonderful time on location, especially with prankster pal director Raoul Walsh to help out. Walsh gave Barbara some lines to say that weren't in the script. They caught Gable by surprise, and he laughed all through the rest of the take and ruined it. Another time, Gable provided some additional lines of his own, which caused Barbara to break up.

Barbara plays Birdie, a former dance hall girl from Chicago, who likes to sing and dance. She's the fluffiest of Jo Van Fleet's daughters-in-law. Three of Van Fleet's bandit sons are all killed while they were robbing a bank. One escapes, but no one knows which. The gold is hidden by their mother, who is guarding the treasure and the sons' four wives in the deserted town of Wagon Mound. When Gable arrives at her farm, Van Fleet shoots him and nurses him back to health, trying to find out what Gable knows about her missing son. While recuperating, Gable charms the girls to find out where the treasure is hidden.

At breakfast, hoping to charm Gable, Birdie sings, "When I was a little girl, I used to play with toys. Now that I'm a bigger girl, I better play with . . . ." She stops singing when she notices that Gable is not at the table but still locked up in his bedroom.

Later on, Birdie entertains Gable with a little song and dance and almost gets him to swim nude with her, which is interrupted thanks to a gunshot warning by Eleanor Parker. Birdie is the only daughter-in-law that doesn't kiss him. When the girls assume Gable has left their farm, Birdie reminisces, "I guess I never would have gotten him anyway, but it sure was fun thinking about it." To which, Van Fleet exclaims, "You're harlots, the lot of ya!"

[64] *Photoplay* magazine, February 1957.

Elaine Hollingsworth, who was then known as Sara Shane, recollects about the filming, "Barbara Nichols and I didn't have any scenes together, other than group shots with the others. Judging by the finished film, I thought she did a good job. Barbara was fun, and really nice, but I hardly knew her, even though we were in the same film. I spent my spare time with Clark's wife, Kay, who was an old friend, and with Eleanor Parker. I didn't get to know Barbara and Jean Willes, not because I didn't like them, but it just didn't happen. That's common on films."[65]

About working under the direction of Raoul Walsh, Elaine recalled, "He was really unpleasant and mean to people who couldn't fight back, but Clark Gable loved him and often used him for his pictures. The rest of us couldn't stand him. He was very mean."

In mid-May and June, interiors were shot at the Samuel Goldwyn studios in Hollywood. Locations were seventeen miles outside St. George, Utah. Nearby, at the Yucca Flats/Nevada Test Site northwest of Las Vegas, near St. George, there had been 87 recent atomic bomb test explosions. Marked increases in cancers were reported from the mid-1950s through 1980. Hundreds of St. George residents filed suit against the federal government, claiming exposure without warning to large doses of radiation.

Whether the cast and crew of *The King and Four Queens* were notified about the possible dangers is unknown. Elaine addressed the issue in an interview years later. "Now, in our film, the cast was rolling around in all that red dust. I was not rolling around in the red dust in our film because I played kind of a staid character who wouldn't be rolling around. Jo Van Fleet died of cancer. Barbara Nichols died of cancer. Jean Willes died of cancer. Now, I don't say it was this, but they'd been doing the atomic testing shortly before we got up there. It is rather curious."[66]

The film received a split reception upon its release on December 21. Barbara received a flattering review in one newspaper: "The rest of the small cast is competent, especially Barbara Nichols, a comparative newcomer, who

[65] Source: email contact with author.
[66] Michael Barnum. www.classicimages.com.

has an especially nice flair for comedy," while others were less positive: "Clark Gable may still be regarded as the 'king' of Hollywood stars, but he won't be for long if he continues to appear in pictures such as *The King and Four Queens*. The greater part of the picture is taken up with his padding among the dames, blinking his eyes, smoothing his whiskers and trying to worm a little information out of each in turn. This is a very tedious business, mainly because the dames are depressingly dull and Mr. Gable is not over-endowed with nerve."[67]

In July and August 1956, Barbara was seen around town regularly with British-born actor, Michael Rennie (1909-1971). He was known around Hollywood as a womanizer.

Pin-up model Jeanne Carmen describes in her memoirs a meeting with Rennie that explains his "big" reputation as a ladies' man.

Barbara described him as ". . . intelligent, sophisticated. He knows his way around."

Columnist Earl Wilson revealed that Rennie took Barbara to the Tijuana bullfights.

"Everything about the bullfights was fascinating," Barbara reports, "especially Michael . . . ." Rennie and Barbara dated for quite a while, but eventually broke up their relationship. In July 1957, Barbara commented on the breakup. "All those crazy lookin' chicks callin' all the time. Phone always ringin'. That's not for me."[68]

Barbara attended the premiere of *Beyond a Reasonable Doubt* on September 5, 1956. Directly after the premiere, she was sent off with Sara Shane and Jean Willes on an eight-week cross-country tour to promote *The King and Four Queens*.

Late October, she returned to Huntington Station and moved in with her parents. Soon afterwards she found a place of her own, an apartment situated nearby 52nd Street and Broadway.

The next year, because she had to travel between New York and Hollywood

---

[67] *The New York Times*, December 2, 1956.
[68] *Lowell Sunday*, July 21, 1957.

for work, she also bought a condo in a three-story apartment off the Sunset Strip in Los Angeles.

In autumn 1956, Barbara took driving lessons, but by early November, she flunked her driving test because she couldn't park the car. By late November, she passed the test and earned her license.

In October 1956, Warner Bros. offered Barbara a small part in *Bombers B-52* (1957). She wanted to play the part of a girl sitting at a bar with her boyfriend, who was staring at television. The part ordered her to keep poking the guy with her elbow and squawking, "I wanna go home!" Barbara thought it could be a very funny bit, but her agent wouldn't let her play it.

When *The King and Four Queens* had its premiere showing at the Mayfair Theatre in New York, on December 21, Barbara sent a chauffeur-driven limousine to pick up her parents for the event. Although anxious to see her daughter's latest movie, Mrs. Nickerauer declined the trip. She told her disappointed daughter that she'd rather wait for the movie to come to Huntington. George and Julia Nickerauer did attend the movie's premiere at the Huntington Theatre on Friday January 18, 1957.

Barbara with Jean Willes, Sara Shane, Clark Gable and Eleanor Parker, 1956.

Barbara with Clark Gable in *The King and Four Queens*, 1956.

Barbara dancing with Clark Gable in *The King and Four Queens*, 1956.

Publicity photo, 1956.

Publicity photo, 1956.

The Sweet Smell of Success

WITH TWO POPULAR STAGE SHOWS and appearances in two quality A pictures on her resume, Barbara's face and talent was now sought after and appreciated by producers looking to cast a "brazen but dumb broad" part. Barbara didn't mind being typecast, although she realized that being categorized would eventually limit her career possibilities. Until then, she enjoyed her moment of fame.

In December 1956 and at the beginning of the New Year, Barbara worked on the Warner Bros. soundstage again. Barbara felt that the studios was a kind of second home. During the filming of *The Pajama Game,* she became the hit of the writer's table in their Green Room, when she came in one day carrying her oversized bags, in which she could never find what she wanted. The writers started kidding her about it, and because of her witty remarks, Barbara ate lunch at their table every day during filming.

In *The Pajama Game,* Barbara played Poopsie, a worker of the Sleeptite Pajama Factory. The story is about a labor furor over a 7.5 ¢ pay raise that complicates the course of true love for Sid Sorokin (John Raitt), the new factory superintendent, and Babe Williams (Doris Day), the feisty employee heading the Union Grievance Committee.

Directly after the titles rolled, Barbara is seen in full frame behind her sewing machine, singing the first two words—"hurry up"—of the song, "Racing With the Clock." She's also featured in the "I'm Not at All in Love" show number with Doris Day, and she has a couple of lines while the girls are having a lunch break, sitting at the stairs in the factory. Beside her participation in several show numbers, Barbara has not much else to do than to follow the conversations of the other cast members in a couple of scenes. Her character doesn't develop beyond that of a dumb blonde.

Barbara got along well with actress Doris Day and her other co-stars, but columnist Dorothy Killgallen reported that there was no love lost between Barbara and Stanley Donen, the movie's director. Donen was not amused when Barbara showed up with purple hair one day, declaring, "I guess the hairdresser got the wrong rinse." Donen made her wear a scarf for the day's scenes.

Maybe Barbara was too outspoken for Donen, something he couldn't handle all that well, for he also had to deal with accusations of speeding up the filming procedures and being sloppy with them. A rumor reached the set that Donen was getting $1,000 a day for every day that he came in ahead of schedule.

Besides these rumors, Donen had declared that he wanted the original Broadway cast for the film version. He almost had the whole cast. Doris Day—who replaced Janis Paige—and Barbara were added to the other players, who reprised their Broadway parts. Tony Award-winning actress Rae Allen (1926) had played the part of Poopsie on Broadway. Doris Day felt insecure about

Donen's wish to make the movie with the original cast. She called the filming of the movie an arduous assignment, because she had to fit into a polished company that had been together for two years.

Rehearsals for *The Pajama Game* began on November 1. Due to an accident on set with Doris, rehearsals were interrupted until November 28.

Stanley Donen's self interest in finishing the picture ahead of schedule proved relentless. The day after Christmas, the entire company had to make up for a day off, and worked from 5 p.m. until 4 a.m. What happened was that, because of extreme fatigue, Carol Haney had collapsed on set, and Doris ordered that she was taken to the hospital. Carol didn't return until January 14. The filming of *The Pajama Game* was completed in mid-February 1957.

Because Barbara was such a quick study, had a good comedy insight and good timing, she had become quite popular on the set. She also pleased the crew with her New Year's card—a photograph of herself in a tailcoat and top hat.

She wore several skin-tight costumes in the movie. "I wouldn't say my costume was too snug, but when the director asked me to close my eyes, it was the most exercise I've had since I played basketball in high school."

Barbara's wisecracking remarks became her trademark. Her personality selling worked, and soon newspapers and magazines picked up stories of her as a zany, say-it-all blonde.

Barbara's husband hunt was a well-featured item in many newspaper columns. According to sources, her mother just wanted her to give up her career, get married, and settle down. Barbara made a joke of it when she told columnist Earl Wilson, "What I really want is a man. So, I called up everybody I used to know. Some of the guys I called—their wives answered."[69]

Probably one of Barbara's finest movie roles was as Rita, a cigarette-selling B-girl, in *Sweet Smell of Success*. The film gives a snapshot of a time in the 1950s, when the dog-eat-dog world of entertainment in New York and people you trusted would betray you if there was a payoff to them in the end. The film tells the story of powerful newspaper columnist J. J. Hunsecker

[69] *Lowell Sunday Sun,* July 21, 1957.

(Burt Lancaster), who uses a small time public relations man, (Tony Curtis) to ruin his sister's relationship with a man he deems inappropriate. Burt does this by dangling a promise to Tony in front of him that he'll make mention of one of his clients in his nationally syndicated newspaper column, which Tony really needs since his success as a public relations man is going downhill and he's losing all his clients. In turn, Tony uses Rita, who works in the nightclub where they conduct business.

Before *Sweet Smell of Success* began filming, Barbara was having an affair with James Hill (1916-2001), who was also one of the film's four producers.

The production of *Sweet Smell of Success* was hazardous, especially when writer Ernest Lehman fell ill and screenwriter Clifford Odets had a hard time rewriting scenes. Many times, the actors were given their lines the day they were about to shoot their scenes. Burt's annoyance with these proceedings made him brood, which led to aggressive outbursts. The director and several cast members were intimidated by his behaviour.

Barbara had two scenes with Sidney the press agent (Tony Curtis), who was Rita's boyfriend and all too willing to "share" her for a higher rung on the ladder of success. Even though Rita makes clear that she is not "that sort of girl," Sidney talks her into spending the night with a columnist she pretends not to know.

That scene is played with special effectiveness by Barbara. As a reaction to Curtis' persuasion to do him a favour, Rita yells, "Don't you think I have any feeling? What am I? A bowl of fruit? A tangerine that peels in a minute?" She finally does give in, and when Sidney leaves, it becomes clear that she already met the columnist in Palm Springs, two years earlier. "Don't tell Sidney," she asks the columnist, while he lights her a fire.

The interiors were shot, with a couple of exceptions, in February and March 1957 at the Goldwyn Studios in Hollywood. *Sweet Smell of Success* was the movie Barbara was proudest of. She finally got the chance to show that she could play more than a sexy, wisecracking blonde bimbo. "Up until I made *Sweet Smell of Success*, I used to do comedy, you know, and I like to do comedy, but in *Sweet Smell of Success,* I play kind of a dramatic part, which is kind of a change of pace for me, which is very nice."[70]

In another interview, she commented on the part of Rita.: "Me, I observe people. I liked the part in *Sweet Smell of Success.* It was someone real. I try to bring dimension to anyone I play. As for sex appeal, I think it comes from inside. It doesn't have anything to do with how you look."[71]

Sweet Smell of Success premiered in New York at Loew's State in Times Square on June 27. Upon its release, the movie was rejected by the public. Audiences disliked seeing their favorite actors in such unsympathetic roles. The producers were fearful that the film's $1.3 million cost would not be recovered. However, *Time* magazine and *The New York Herald* included the film on their Top 10 list for 1957.

The New York Times mentioned Barbara in its review. " . . . and Barbara Nichols, as the voluptuous nightclub temptress Mr. Curtis uses in his schemes; Sam Levene, as an agent; Joe Frisco, as a comic, and Jeff Donnell, as Mr. Curtis' harried secretary add competent touches in their brief appearances."[72]

Boxoffice Magazine was also enthusiastic about Barbara's performance. "Barbara Nichols, a pathetic little cigarette girl forced to play up to men customers she dislikes, contributes one of the picture's most moving scenes."[73]

Burt Lancaster and Barbara later appeared together in a comedy sketch on *The Ed Sullivan Show* as part of the publicity tour for the movie. The show was broadcast from the Outdoor Marine Theatre at Jones Beach, New York, on June 23.

Barbara was grateful to producer Burt Lancaster, for giving her the chance to show she was a competent dramatic actress. He was very satisfied with her performance, and their personalities clicked. Barbara became close friends with him and his wife, Norma Anderson. (Their friendship lasted until Burt

---

[70] *TV's Tabloid,* July 3, 1957.

[71] *TV Guide,* July 23-29, 1960.

[72] June 28, 1957.

[73] *Boxoffice Magazine,* June 29, 1957

and Norma divorced in 1969. Many biographies and publications about Burt mention the cause of the divorce being Norma's alcoholism.)

In 1958, Burt's daughter, Joanna, made Barbara an honorary member of the Bellagio's School's Parents Teacher's Association.

When Hedda Hopper asked Barbara about her closest friends in Hollywood, she answered, "The Burt Lancasters; they've been very nice to me. I love their kids. I think Norma and Burt are the greatest. Mike Connelly is a good friend of mine. I don't really have so many friends, you know."[74]

A striking anecdote about Barbara is told in Burt's biography by author Kate Buford. She describes how screenwriter Ernest Lehman was asked to write a note to accompany three dozen roses that James Hill had ordered for Barbara. After interviewing, wining, dining, and sleeping with her, Hill had left her apartment at 2 a.m. Outside her building, he met a woman walking her dog. She took him back in with her, and while in bed with that woman, Barbara interrupted their liaison. "Barbara, a friend of the woman, showed up ready to have a girl-talk visit in the middle of the night, saw Hill, and got 'hysterical.'"[75]

Both James Hill and Burt Lancaster were alcoholics, and they shared their women. Barbara was willing to play the field, but refused to be used. Several years later, she told her friend, Paula Stewart, that she had had an affair with Burt in the late 1960s. Paula said, "His picture hung over her bed! According to her, they had an affair. Barbara didn't pussyfoot around. She was very sexual."[76]

---

[74] Unpublished notes from an interview with Hedda Hopper. Dated 4-10-1958.

[75] Buford, Kate. *Burt Lancaster: An American Life*. New York: Random House, Inc., 2000.

[76] Source: email contact with author.

Barbara on the set of *The Pajama Game* with Eddie Foy Jr., John Raitt and Doris Day, 1957.

Barbara with Doris Day and chorus in *The Pajama Game*, 1957.

Barbara with Jack Straw and Thelma Pelish in *The Pajama Game*, 1957.

Barbara on the set of *Sweet Smell of Success*, 1957.

Barbara and Tony Curtis in *Sweet Smell of Success*, 1957.

Barbara and Tony Curtis in *Sweet Smell of Success*, 1957.

Barbara and David White in *Sweet Smell of Success*, 1957.

Barbara and poodle Hifi.

An inscribed photograph by Burt Lancaster. (Courtesy of Janice Pease).

Nichols versus Mansfield, Monroe, and Novak

DIRECTLY AFTER THE FILMING of *Sweet Smell of Success* was completed, Barbara reported to Columbia Pictures studios to start working on the film version of *Pal Joey*. Beginning in March 1957, filming ran over eight weeks in total, with most major scenes completed by the end of May. The film starred Frank Sinatra as Joey Evans, Rita Hayworth, and her pretender to the Columbia throne, blonde Kim Novak.

The press expected fireworks between Rita and Kim, but that didn't happen. The two actresses worked pleasantly together. However, that was not the case with Kim and Barbara. Kim detested the role of showgirl Linda English and had a hard time getting in character. Barbara soon became fed up with her work ethics. She commented to the press, "She doesn't like me, and the feeling is mutual. Working with her is a drag. She's the most unprofessional show business person I've met."

Another point of irritation for Barbara was the fact that she had to change the color of her hair, because Kim's shade was the same. Kim told director George Sidney to urge Barbara to change voluntarily, but when she refused, Kim appealed to a higher authority, and an order came down from studio boss Harry Cohn. Eventually, Barbara ended up with a brassier hue. As a result, the two actresses didn't speak off-camera for the duration of filming.

Barbara played the gum-chewing showgirl, Gladys. She dislikes Joey from the first time she lays eyes on him, and she tells him so.

"I heard about you, buster. My sister worked with you in Fresno. She told me all about you."

Joey remarks, "Which one was she?"

"The one you didn't get to first base with."

"Oh, she was the ugly one. Must be twins."

Barbara was given good dialogue and was featured in several scenes with Frank Sinatra. About working with him, she said, "Frank Sinatra is lots of laughs. Of course, he does everything in one take. In comedy I think too much rehearsal can spoil it."

For her part, Barbara had to rehearse several dance numbers and had a hard time learning the moves. Dancer Christopher Riordan said, "My friend, Hermes Pan, who choreographed her in *Pal Joey*, told me it was difficult to 'train her' as he put it. She was not a dancer. Yes, she could move, but she didn't know the terms, and she had a hard time concentrating on the routine."[77]

While Kim Novak was to play Linda, a dreamy showgirl with morals, Barbara was again type cast as the tough cookie chorine, Cladys. When Linda is in rehearsal for a striptease number that Joey talked her into, Gladys is looking on. Joey suddenly stops the number and orders Linda to go to the dressing room and to put her clothes on. Turning to Gladys, he tells her the number is hers.

---

[77] Source: email contact with author.

"A pleasure," Gladys replies, while she walks to the stage to rehearse her new number.

To a sobbing Linda, Joey explains, "A nice girl is a nice girl anywhere. I shouldn't have let you do it."

Barbara commented about being typecast. "I don't mind, though, playing sexy characters all the time, I mean. Even in sexy parts you get a chance to show you can act. I have no ambition to play *Brothers Karamazov*, but I would like roles that are a little serious now and then. I like comedy, too. My aim is to get the kind of parts they give Shelley Winters. She looks half-sexy, if you know what I mean."[78]

Just like *The Pajama Game*, in *Pal Joey* there isn't much to do for Barbara in the few scenes she has. Her show number—as seen in the lobby card set of the movie—was cut from the final print. Still, she leaves a memorable impression in her scenes with Frank Sinatra, showing her talent as an actress and comedienne.

Although Barbara had proven in her performances on television and on the big screen that she was a talented actress and comedienne, she was not considered star material by Hollywood producers. The blonde bimbo personality she had been selling was becoming a barrier against being assigned for leading roles in Hollywood productions. Unlike Monroe and Mansfield, to which she now was constantly compared, Barbara's agent only could get her co-starring parts in films. Barbara acted nonchalant about it when she told columnist Earl Wilson, "I'm not one of these dedicated dames. If I don't get movie jobs, so all right, I'll work in a five-and-dime."[79]

In a newspaper interview with Harry Harris, Barbara explains why she doesn't like to be one of the sexy blondes. She describes that only one of them, Marilyn Monroe, has talent, and that the others have only saleable personalities. Barbara ranked Marilyn first in the beauty department. "She has a kind of sweet baby face." Second is Kim Novak, though Barbara adds that "she has a bad figure and no talent." Third and fourth are Zsa Zsa Gabor and

[78] *The Miami News*, July 18, 1957.
[79] July 20, 1957.

Marie Wilson. Fifth and sixth are Mamie Van Doren and Jayne Mansfield. Barbara said "they try to look like Marilyn, but they don't succeed." When asked by Harris where she would rank herself, Barbara protested. "That's not fair. I try to look only like me. Besides, I don't think I'm like those girls. Really I don't. I don't want to do that kind of part."[80]

Although Barbara didn't like to be ranked in the same division as her blonde contemporaries, she didn't dislike Jayne or Marilyn completely, as the press were stating. Barbara's psychic John Cohan said, "Barbara liked Monroe and Mansfield for they worked hard to get to where they were in the industry, but Barbara felt she was a far better serious actress than those two in drama stuff."[81]

Only on rare occasions, Barbara showed that she was fed up with the comparison. While appearing as a guest in the Canadian TV show, *Tabloid*, on July 3, 1957, its host, Dick MacDougal, barely got her to crack a smile. From her facial expressions, it is clear that she gets irritated at the questions asked about her likeness to Jayne Mansfield. She answers MacDougal, "I don't see any resemblance. I don't like to be compared with anyone else, I would like to think that I am Barbara Nichols. And Jayne Mansfield is Jayne Mansfield. I don't like to be compared with anyone else."

MacDougal goes on and asks her what she thinks are the similarities in her career and that of Marilyn and Jayne. "There are studio-made actresses and there are actresses that have made it on their own, so to speak. First of all, I'm *not* on a contract to anyone and I've worked in New York on the Broadway stage, I have done summer stock and live television. And my quotes are my own, the studio didn't make them up." Unintentionally Barbara described herself with a description that for the most part perfectly fit the persona and career of Jayne Mansfield, too.

One year later, Barbara lashed out at blonde actresses Dagmar and Jayne Mansfield again. "I won't go for that [playing the dumb blonde type]. I have

---

[80] *The Philadelphia Inquirer*, July 30, 1957.

[81] Source: email contact with author.

never thought Jayne Mansfield or Dagmar were sexy. They're too obvious."[82] Still Barbara had accepted parts that would type-cast her as a Monroe-like movie star. In an episode of TV's *Dragnet* called "The Big Star," she played a Hollywood glamour girl, who receives anonymous extortion letters, threatening to disfigure her unless she comes up with a huge sum of money. She called her character "... dumb, like Jayne Mansfield."

John Cohan, who also counted Jayne Mansfield among his clients, states, "Barbara didn't hate Jayne Mansfield but stayed clear many times, for Jayne caught her husband Mickey in bed with Barbara. As career women, they liked, admired each other, but Mickey created the rift between them."[83]

Barbara's fling with Mickey Hargitay probably happened in the early 1960s, when the two actresses had appeared in *The George Raft Story* (1961). At the time, Jayne and Mickey were having marital problems, mainly because Jayne was having affairs with other men. Jayne's press agent, Ray Strait, remembered that Barbara specifically did not care for Mickey. She considered him crude. He recalled that she liked Jayne better. "What I do know is that Barbara had a 'thing' for Jayne. Whether it resulted in anything, I don't know except that Jayne was quite fond of her and they did have a couple of girls' nights out together."[84]

Early July, 1957, Barbara's parents were quite surprised when she drove up to their house in a chauffeured limousine and took them and a neighbor, Mrs. Kay Petrone, to dinner and several nightclubs. For Barbara, this night out was one of the rare occasions to get her parents to leave their hometown. They attended the opening of her latest movie at the Shore Theatre. The reason Barbara was in town was to promote the movie. She enjoyed being the toast of New York because of her role in *Sweet Smell of Success*.

One evening, she and her friends had been visiting a nightclub and were feted by an admirer who had sent her a bottle of wine. The party went on till

---

[82] *Mirror News*, June 9, 1958.

[83] Source: email contact with author.

[84] Source: email contact with author.

the early hours. Sleeping in the next day made her lose her reserved table in a restaurant to Marilyn Monroe's ex-husband, baseball player Joe DiMaggio.

Besides visiting her parents, she also visited her grandmother and an aunt and uncle during her time in Huntington. She also took time to catch up with old friends. One of those visits changed Barbara's rise to stardom drastically.

Barbara with Frank Sinatra and chorus in *Pal Joey*, 1957.

THAT KIND OF WOMAN

Barbara and Kim Novak in *Pal Joey*, 1957.

Barbara between takes with Frank Sinatra. (Courtesy of Janice Pease).

Barbara with Frank Sinatra in *Pal Joey*, 1957. (Courtesy of Janice Pease).

Barbara in TV's *Dragnet*, 1957.

Casualty and Recognition

ON JULY 26, 1957, Barbara had been invited to visit friends Leverett Saltonstall Miller—a millionaire polo player—and a former movie starlet/model, Ava Norring, at their summer home in Syosset, New York. On their way back to Huntington Station, their car crashed head-on into the car of Roland Tetrault. Barbara was severely injured.

Columnist Dorothy Killgallen mentioned, "...while her host was driving her out, faulty brakes caused a crash on the Jericho Turnpike."

Barbara was admitted into Meadowbrook Hospital. At first, doctors thought she had suffered only minor bruises and a concussion, but her condition became worse, and an emergency operation was performed to remove her spleen and sew up parts of a lacerated kidney. She received several blood transfusions and was fed with a tube extended through her nose to her stomach, right after the operation.

Barbara received messages and attention from a lot of people, shocked by the news of her accident, "I got messages from everybody; newspaper people, everybody. Warner Bros. sent flowers and plants. It made me feel good. I don't know what I've done without that. I learned how to knit and all that. I go crazy when I'm not working anyway. I have to be busy all the time."

On July 30, a newspaper reported that Barbara was in fair condition. For weeks, she hovered between life and death. She spent almost a year in the care of her parents, while recuperating from the accident. Her convalescence was long and painful.

The same determination and willpower that carried her to stardom prevailed. A year later, she resumed her film career. In an interview Barbara had after the accident, she said, "I'm very lucky to be here. I'd just finished *Pal Joey* and left next day for the personal appearance tour. So, I missed quite a few pictures."

Miller, Norring, and both occupants of the second car were treated for cuts and bruises. Barbara had met Ava Norring around 1952 when both were modeling for photographer Bruno Bernard, also known as Bernard of Hollywood. Late July, Ava and Barbara were involved in a publicity stunt, when they were jailed for wearing bikinis on the Jacob Riis Park boardwalk, in Queens, New York. A tense moment in their friendship occurred in September 1958, when Barbara sued the Millers for $1 million. She alleged that she sustained injuries because of the negligence of Mr. Tetrault and Leverett S. Miller, while riding in the latter's car to be their weekend guest.

A year earlier, she was reported talking to her lawyers about suing producers Hecht, Hill, and Lancaster, because of the injuries she contracted in another car accident while she was making personal appearances for them to publicize the movie *Sweet Smell of Success* (1957). The Miller vs. Nichols case was settled in February 1961; Barbara received several thousand dollars insurance as a settlement. Why she tried to cash in on the accidents is unknown. The Millers and Lancasters were her friends, and, after recuperating, she continued her career successfully.[85]

Partly because her agent couldn't find her good leading parts, Barbara decided to shift her focus from moviemaking to stage and television work. She stated that she preferred the freedom of being a freelance actor instead of being under contract to a film studio. "When you sign one of those long picture deals, they don't let you do television or much of anything else. No thanks, I like to work, and I don't play tennis. In Hollywood, if you're not working, you've got to play tennis. Nothing else to do."

A July newspaper article headlined "Nichols shuns movies for TV." The article mentioned that Barbara "will never stray far from the medium that brought her fame." She explained. "I owe it all to television. Last year, when Warner Bros. asked me to fly to the coast and make a test, my agent sent a kinescope of a Sid Caesar show in which I appeared. As a result, the studio signed me without my having to make the test. How could you help but feel grateful to an industry that does that for you!"[86] The writer of the article, Marie Torre, concluded, "Thus, it shouldn't surprise anyone to know that television has something to do with Barbara's firm decision to avoid long-term movie deals, such as the seven-year contract her friend Jayne Mansfield has with 20th Century Fox. Barbara doesn't envy Jayne at all for that arrangement."

Maybe Barbara's declaration of love for TV resulted in a leading part in the *Kraft Theatre* episode, "Sextuplets." She told *New York Herald Tribune* reporter Torre in that same interview, "I'm going to play a hillbilly with six children. It's actually a sort of Daisy Mae role, you might say. I'm supposed to have an Ozark accent."

In mid-July, Barbara was signed for the show, but she was unable to follow up on the agreement because of the car accident on July 27. Actress Tammy Grimes was signed instead. The part of the hillbilly mother was quite

---

[85] Ava Norring (1929-2016) was struggling with dementia when I contacted her daughter Maria-Flora. Miss Norring told her daughter that she wasn't in the car at the time of the accident. She did remember Barbara fondly.

[86] *The Miami News*, July 18, 1957.

a loss for Barbara. It would have been her first starring role in her career, and her first married woman role.

Recuperation took time, and Barbara needed plastic surgery because a scar that she received prevented her from bending over forward. She was thought to have said, "That'd put me out of work!"

In mid-August, she was discharged by her doctors, and she and her mother planned a rest at the seashore.

The Pajama Game had its premiere at Radio City Music Hall in New York on August 30, but Barbara was unable to attend.

She resumed her acting career when she took a part in Warner Bros. Television Western series, *Maverick*. She only agreed to play the part of gang member Michael Dante's girlfriend, Blanche, if she would not be involved in too much physical labor.

Dante (1931) remembered her as: ". . . a beautiful woman with a great sense of humor and a good actress. Very underrated. She left us much too soon." About her physical condition he recalled, "The director made sure she didn't do anything physical. She was a professional, one would not know she was recently in an auto accident. She was a very good, loveable person. She was a joy to work with, I'll always remember her infectious laugh."[87]

In September, Barbara was cheered along the road to recovery when she learned that Nat Hiken, the writer-producer that created Sgt. Bilko in *The Phil Silvers Show* (1955-1959), thought that she was "a beauty, a good actress, and excellent comedienne." He tried to work her into the series, but that never happened.

Barbara was signed for a recurring role in the sitcom, *Love That Jill*, which was to start filming at the end of the year. The show was originally tagged *Jacques and Jill*, and starred real-life husband and wife Robert Sterling and Anne Jeffreys as managers of opposing model agencies in New York City. Jill constantly tries to steal Jack Gibson's business opportunities, and conjures some comical ways in which to do so.

---

[87] Source: email contact with author.

Barbara appeared regularly as Ginger, a ditsy blonde, who start out working for Jill and switched to working for Jack.

Actress Melinda Markey (1934) had a guest part in one episode. "I remember it vaguely; it was not a highlight in my career, I would say. I remember Barbara Nichols. I got along fine with her. She was easy to work with, no problems. The show was not very well received."[88]

Critic Harry Harris watched the new show and was appalled. "Last night at 8, ABC switched programs, from Guy's to Doll's—from Guy Mitchell's live variety show—to Anne Jeffreys' filmed situation comedy, *Love That Jill*. The change was not for the better. The new entry is dime-a-dozen Hollywood hokum." A brief mentioning of Barbara didn't make things better. "There were several instances of exaggerated hip-wiggling, generous views of Barbara Nichols as a fought-over model, and number of coy attempts at 'naughty' talk. But these hardly ended up to an 'adult eastern.'"[89]

The New York Times October 1, 1957 issue mentioned that Vincent Price and Barbara had been assigned the leading roles in the Harry Essex-Joseph Ruscoll play, *A Neighborhood Affair*. Producers Richard W. Krakauer and Joseph Justman placed the play in rehearsal in December.

Barbara was seen dining out with Krakauer at the El Morocco in October, and in November, she was back in Hollywood to confer with Essex about her part in the play. Unfortunately, the play never saw the light of day, and Barbara moved on to other things.

When her agent had landed her three small parts in quality A pictures, Barbara must have gotten the feeling that she had to start her film career all over again. In January 1958, she started working on *Ten North Frederick*, filming a scene with Gary Cooper. She received $1,000 for one day of work. Filmed at 20th Century Fox, the wardrobe department fitted Barbara in the polka dot dress that Marilyn Monroe had worn in *The Seven Year Itch* (1955). Barbara's scene was originally seven minutes long, but was cut to half for the

---

[88] Source: telephone conversation with author, 8-12-2015.

[89] *The Philadelphia Inquirer*, January 21, 1958.

final print, because she had created the required mood in an incredibly brief time. "Two minutes of Barbara Nichols on screen can do it," producer Charles Brackett exclaimed. "I must have her for the part."[90]

Barbara plays Stella, a party girl. She meets a drunken Cooper when she knocks on the wrong hotel door. The two make themselves comfortable. When he assumes that Stella is selling herself, she feels insulted, at first, but flirts with him at the same time.

Film Bulletin reviewed the movie and found Barbara to be "A peroxide potato . . . who is all the tintyped squeals and inanities you've ever been led to expect."[91]

Barbara found Gary Cooper to be "real nice, kind of like a little boy." She was also impressed with working at 20th Century Fox and their makeup department in particular. "At some studios, I wouldn't let them go near my hair," she said, "they give the impression they don't really care unless you are the star." Makeup artist Ben Nye and hair stylist Helen Turpin had worked with Jayne Mansfield and Marilyn Monroe on several occasions before they worked with Barbara. (The couple would groom Barbara again in 1959 for *Woman Obsessed*.)

On February 3, *Boxoffice* magazine mentioned that Barbara was signed for the leading female role in *The Naked and the Dead*, a film based on Norman Mailer's novel that starred Aldo Ray and Cliff Robertson. Later that month, she reported to the RKO Radio Pictures studio to work two weeks. She commented on her role that it was another sexy part. "All I wear, honey, is some black lace and an old kimono left over from *Sayonara*." Actor James Best (1926-2015) played the small part of a soldier. He remembered Barbara as "friendly on the set and a lovely lady."[92]

Aldo Ray was drunk during the entire production. Distribution of *The Naked and the Dead* was taken over from failing RKO by Warner Bros. That

---

[90] *Chicago Sunday Tribune*, June 1, 1958.
[91] *Film Bulletin*, April 28, 1958.
[92] Source: email contact with author.

studio tried to make the film more commercially appealing by adding some romantic subplots involving a striptease artist played by Lili St. Cyr and a promiscuous wife named Mildred, played by Barbara. Director Raoul Walsh was ordered by Jack Warner to "put some tits in the movie."[93]

The female characters only appear in brief flashbacks during the film. The first flashback scene shows the newly married Mildred and Sam Croft lying in the hay in a barn, making out. In the second flashback, Sergeant Sam Croft returns home from the war and finds his wife, Mildred, hastily putting on a dressing gown. As he bursts in on her lover, she yells, "Sam, don't hit him. He's from the finance company!" She tells her fleeting lover to phone her later and yells at her husband, "You big ham. You spoiled everything!" To which, Sam hits her.

The New York Times reviewer wrote, "The adaption, which does not always adhere to the book, concentrates on typing each man. One is the ill-fated Sergeant Croft, who is explained, is driven by an overweening urge to command because of the memory of an unfaithful wife. From his actions, however one is led to think that he just likes killing. The other members of the detail are competent, but also appear to have been chosen solely to represent the types that compromised our citizen army. Their women, namely Lili St. Cyr, as the stripper; Barbara Nichols, as Mr. Ray's voluptuous, two-timing wife, and a covey of cuties recalled by the platoon's lieutenant only pass briefly in review."

There was one bad note amid the acclaim Barbara got because of her movie acting. Aired on May 29, 1958, TV's *Climax* gave her one of her first bad reviews. Judging her acting in the episode, "The Push-Button Giant," one critic called Barbara "A spectacularly endowed young lady, but possibly the worst actress ever seen on TV."

Another didn't put the blame solely on Barbara, declaring that, "A more confused and inept script would take a lot of looking for, so the perfunctory performances by [Barry] Nelson and such other ordinarily dependable players

---

[93] www.americanlegends.com

as Everett Sloane, Bob Sweeney, Martha Hyer, and Barbara Nichols were probably good—or bad—enough."[94]

Although there were more critics that were sceptical about her acting skills and categorized her in the glamour doll department, Barbara was still happy with the way her career was going. She didn't show any sign of disappointment to the press and public, when she attended the star-studded midnight premiere of *Ten North Frederick* in Santa Barbara. Along with Maureen O'Hara, Yvonne De Carlo, Nick Adams, and other stars, Barbara went aboard the train that 20th Century Fox hired to travel from Hollywood to Santa Barbara.

In August, a tongue-in-cheek performance on the *Steve Lawrence and Eydie Gormé Show* had Barbara singing "A Little Brains, A Little Talent," ridiculing her critics.

Luckily, Barbara also had several powerful supporters in Hollywood. Besides her friends, Earl Wilson, Mike Connolly, and Burt Lancaster, Clark Gable was a booster for her career by declaring her a talented actress, and he gave her the title of "Hollywood's new Mae West." Feared Hollywood columnist Hedda Hopper proved to be an alliance, too, when she devoted an article about Barbara, titled, "A Surplus Amount of X."[95]

Hedda described Barbara as the most popular blonde "with voluptuous curves and an illicit look' in Hollywood. Barbara was quoted, "But I do wish, before I get too old, I could get a chance to play a big part. I've been lucky to be in all big pictures, but I really haven't had a part that runs through the entire picture. I wish they'd test me for the *Jean Harlow Story* if they're ever going to do it. She wasn't a great beauty, but she was the first of the sexy blondes, and her story should make a great script."

Hedda concluded her article with, "Barbara Nichols has more beauty than Jean Harlow and is a good actress, to boot. But the two have one thing in common—a surplus amount of ingredient X, and I think if she gets a chance to play the role she'll be sensational."

[94] *The Philadelphia Inquirer* May 30, 1958.
[95] *The Pittsburgh Press*, June 1, 1958

Warner Bros. publicity photo.

Peekaboo.

Barbara in *Maverick*, 1958.

Barbara with Nancy Hadley, Claire Kelly and Kaye Elhardt in the episode "Tonight's the Night" of TV's *Love that Jill*, 1958.

Barbara and Gary Cooper in *Ten North Frederick*, 1958.

Barbara and Gary Cooper in *Ten North Frederick*, 1958.

Publicity photo for *Ten North Frederick*, 1958.

Barbara and Joey Bishop, publicity for *The Naked and the Dead*, 1958.

Barbara and Aldo Ray in *The Naked and the Dead*, 1958.

Barbara and Aldo Ray in *The Naked and the Dead*, 1958.

Publicity photo with Aldo Ray, Lily St. Cyr and Cliff Robertson.

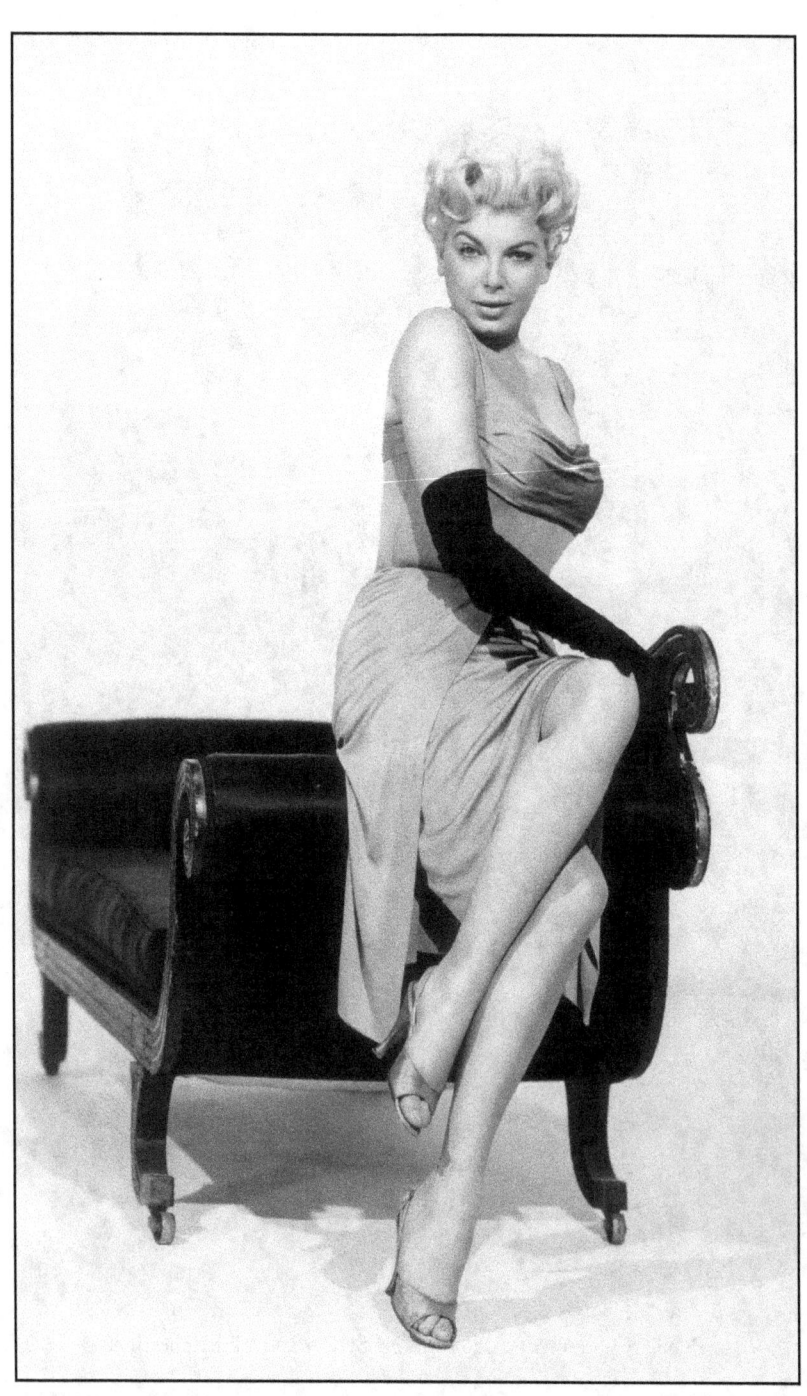

That Kind of Woman

IN THE HOT SUMMER OF 1958, Barbara traveled to her hometown to stay with her parents for the filming of *That Kind of Woman*. She almost lost her role to actress Shirley MacLaine. A June 11, 1958 *Variety* article had listed Shirley in the cast. She was considered for the role of Jane, but Carlo Ponti, producer and husband of the movie's leading actress, Sophia Loren, insisted that a lesser-known actress play the part in order not to overshadow Sophia. Instead, director Sidney Lumet suggested Barbara, to which Ponti agreed.

At the time, actor Tab Hunter (1931) was considered by some critics to be too boyish to play the lead opposite voluptuous, womanly Sophia Loren. However, Tab was happy to play the part of soldier Red.

"I loved doing *That Kind of Woman*. I was under contract at Warner Bros. and they requested me for it, so I went over to meet Sophia and Sidney at Paramount. I really loved doing that movie. It was a very good script and working for Sidney, who was such a perfectionist, is one of the highlights of my career. I was crazy about him, he's a wonderful, wonderful director. He was one of those directors that came from live television. The days of live TV were so important."

On the set, Tab met Barbara. "Barbara Nichols was a wonderful gal. She was always good at playing the friend of the leading lady. I loved her vulnerability, it's a great gift to have and she certainly had that. She worked so well with Sophia. They got along really, really well. They worked together absolutely beautifully. There was just a great contrast, the two of them. Sophia was excellent and Barbara played that character magnificently. She was very close to that character; she was able to project a great deal into that character."[96]

That Kind of Woman was lensed between the end of June and August 13, 1958, in and around New York. Interior scenes were shot in June, location scenes in July. Interiors were filmed at the Gold Medal Studios in the Bronx and Fox Movietone Studios in Manhattan. The scenes set in the Miami train station were actually shot at the Long Beach terminal on Long Island.

Barbara and her fellow cast members rehearsed above Ratner's Deli at 138 Delancey Street on the Lower East Side. Tab Hunter recalled in his autobiography how he loved how dedicated Sidney Lumet was to rehearsals. "His thoroughness really paid off when we started shooting, because we were whisked all over New York."[97]

The drama was placed in summer 1944. Sophia Loren played Kay, the mistress of A. L., a Manhattan millionaire (George Sanders), who uses her to help him influence his contacts at The Pentagon. While en route from Miami to New York City by train, Kay and her friend, Jane (Barbara Nichols), meet Red, an American GI (Tab Hunter) and Kelly, his sergeant and friend (Jack

---

[96] Source: telephone conversation with author, 11-17-2015.

[97] Hunter, Tab with Muller, Eddie. *Tab Hunter Confidential – The Making of a Movie Star*. New York: Algonquin Books of Chapel Hill, 2006.

Warden). Soon entangled in a complicated love affair, Loren has to choose between Sanders and Hunter.

Barbara had several good scenes with Jack and Sophia, and is seen in almost the entire movie. She perfectly portrayed the dim-witted and pathetic Jane, who is eager to hold a man longer than just a couple of dates.

In one of Barbara's scenes, she's with Loren in the powder room of a restaurant where they were invited for dinner by Sanders. She makes a comment on her new date for the evening. "He's not bad at all for a general. He's not fat and he's got a nice smile. If he's got such a nice smile he must be nice all the way through."

Loren replies, "Be happy with the nice smile."

Later on, the girls spend a day out with the two soldiers. Red asks Jane whether she likes Kelly, to which she replies, "I like everybody, it's my nature."

Barbara's finest moment comes at the end, when she says goodbye to Kelly. Heartbroken, she tells him to go, choosing the life of a kept woman to a married man, above true happiness with him. When she leaves for the airport to fly to Washington to live in an apartment arranged by the general, she says goodbye to Kay.

"You're different. You're special. There's nothing for a girl like me. All I am is a good time."

Kay replies that everybody likes a good time.

"But nobody wants to marry one," Jane answers, adding, "You know what I was thinking just now . . . I hope the war never ends. Isn't that awful? All those boys being hurt and killed. I want it to go on and on, just like now. What's going to happen to me when the war ends? What's going to happen to all the good times?"

Actor and talk show host Ron Russell was a bit player in the movie. He recalled working on the film and meeting Barbara. "It was 1958 and I was seventeen years old, a kid who wanted to be in movies. I got in the film as an extra."

Early in the morning, Ron reported to the set. "I got there at five in the morning. Sophia Loren and Barbara had not arrived yet. The crew was setting up the lights and the camera set up. Around six in the morning, a car pulls up and out steps Sophia Loren. I was in shock. She was very tall and big and dark. She had on sunglasses and a trench coat and a scarf over her head tied like a pirate. Not the beauty we saw on the screen. I thought she was okay looking. Soon after, I saw Barbara walking down the train platform. She was in a black knee-length coat with black pointed skinny, very high heels and a black turban on her head. Barbara was almost as tall as I am. I'm six feet tall and she was about five eight or five nine, with those long, long legs and high heels she was almost six feet tall. I guess they hired her because she fit the part and was as tall as Sophia. Sophia did not like to be the tallest one in her films.

"Barbara hadn't any makeup on, just sunglasses. She did not look like her screen persona. She looked tired, like she had been drinking and was up all night. The girls went into their dressing rooms. Tab Hunter arrived and went right into his dressing room. If I remember correctly, the dressing rooms were train cars."

Ron experienced long waits on the set before the stars came out and the cameras started rolling. "After what seemed like years, the film was ready to roll. I was dressed as a soldier and I was told to hang off the train and start waving my arms and yelling at the two beauties that would soon walk down the train platform. Lights, camera, action, and there they were. I thought of Jane Russell and Marilyn Monroe in *Gentlemen Prefer Blondes* when I saw these two hot women: Barbara the platinum blonde and Sophia the dark-haired beauty. They had to walk fast and wiggle and shake their boobs as they walked like two strippers, which was easy for Barbara because she played a stripper many times. Sophia walked like 'here it is but you can't have it.' They walked past us as we whistled and yelled at them. Now, a trick to get the concrete to look better in film is to wet it with water. They did. As Sophia walked down the train station platform she slipped and tripped and fell on her knee. They stopped the film and she went to her dressing room."

While waiting for Sophia to return, Ron took his chance to talk to Barbara. "I made a beeline for Barbara and I introduced myself to her. She was sweet and a bit standoffish. I was then told by one of the jerks who worked for the film not to speak to the stars. I thought to myself, 'Yeah right, fuck off.' I went after her just the same. Barbara listened to what I had to say and I do not remember what that was. I was nervous, but the one thing I do remember was telling her I was gay and not after her body. She laughed and said, 'My best friend is gay and he's after my body.' We both laughed.

"She had a good sense of humor and did, in fact, wisecrack a lot. Knowing that I was gay relaxed her a lot. She may have thought I was hitting on her if I were straight. I asked her if she was from Brooklyn and she answered that she was from Queens. I said, 'I live in Queens, Astoria Queens, but I was born in Brooklyn.' Barbara said she was born in Queens. She had a Queens accent. Wow! I thought now she will be my friend; we are both from Queens. She sat down in her chair that had her name on the back. All kinds of workers were around her. Hair people, make up and a very gay-looking young guy who was showing her how to walk down the platform. From where I was hiding I could see he wanted her to walk faster and to shake her hips from side to side more and to shake her boobs as she was bouncing along. He should have put on her wig (yes, she wore white wigs) and do that scene. He was far more feminine and sexier than she was.

"Filming the scene took several hours, and, around noon, the cast leaves the set to eat and rest. "Now it's lunch time," Ron remembered, "and Sophia disappeared. Barbara was standing talking to a gang of people. I was sneaking around and I stood alongside of the gang of people. She looked at me and smiled and shook her head as to say 'No, no, you're not supposed to be here.' I stayed, and she may have thought I was brave or a fan of hers, and, yes, I was indeed a fan. She turned to me and said, 'Hey Soldier, how long are you going to be on our picture?' I was thrilled and she knew it, too. She was making me feel like it was our picture. She had that kind of caring.

"I was getting used to hearing her voice. It was deep and normal, nothing like when she spoke in that high squeaking voice. She was very kind and understood where I was coming from. She had been there once and remembered what it was like."

About the relationship between Sophia Loren and Barbara, Ron remembered, "I did get the feeling that Sophia snubbed Barbara because Barbara looked like a hooker or a stripper. I don't think Sophia knew how many films and TV Barbara had made and that she was a very well-known actress in America."

Ron concluded, "At the end of my day shoot, I kissed Barbara on the cheek, and she giggled and said, 'Good luck, kid.' I also had the nerve to ask Sophia for a kiss, and she did. She kissed me on my cheek. I went to my cousin's house and I told her all about my day's work. I did make my role in the film a little more important than it was, almost like the co-stars, but I was seventeen and in love with filmmaking. I still am and I still work but not as an extra. Now I'm never told not to speak to the stars."[98]

Another teenager also got the chance to meet Barbara on the set. Nineteen-year-old Anita Leone was spotted by Barbara among the many teenagers that showed up at the Long Beach railroad station to see the actors film a scene. Her father, Reynold Leone, ran a restaurant across the street from the shooting location at Long Beach station and he invited the entire movie company to dinner. They came to lunch instead, and Anita wangled an invitation to dine with the stars. Then Barbara said, 'Isn't that strange? I saw that cute little blond in the crowd and mentioned to Sophia that I'd be interested in getting her for my understudy.' Barbara got Leone the job, and the young girl reported to the set.

Anita recalled, "All they did was have light meters on my face and my hair. The stars acted out the scene once and then everything Barbara did I had to do—every little move. We did it over and over again. Barbara was wonderful to me. She gave me a pep talk and said, 'You did wonderfully.'" Anita served as Barbara's stand-in for the duration of filming and received a daily salary of $22.50.

Mike Connolly, Barbara's friend, implied in his newspaper that there had been a feud between Barbara and Sophia Loren. He suggested that Sophia declined to wear the 1940s fashion and pageboy hairdo, sticking to

---

[98] Source: email contact with author.

contemporary fashion styles. He wrote, "Barbara, the second femme lead, was stuck with what she started with. I saw it with her. She cried through most of the unreeling—and not because it's a sad plot!"[99]

Although *That Kind of Woman* received fairly positive reviews, it failed at the box office. *The New York Times* mentioned that "The two credible characters in it are Jack Warden as a slangy, tough G.I., and Keenan Wynn as a hawk-eyed chaperone for the 'keptive and for Barbara Nichols as a caricature of a 'doll'."

TV Guide magazine praised Barbara's acting. "Very little rings true in the picture except for the Nichols character—an insecure and promiscuous young woman—who unfortunately isn't given enough screen time."

Film critic Barbara Cloud said, "Barbara Nichols, a dizzy blond type who has managed to combine a shapely torso AND talent." She also mentions that Jack Warden and Barbara rescue more than one scene from a series of yawns.[100]

Feared gossip columnist Louella Parsons wrote, "Barbara Nichols has been hiding her light under a bushel. Suddenly she comes up as a fine actress. She's very good in *That Kind of Woman*."

In a May 1960 interview in *The New York Times*, Sidney Lumet, who had received praise for his work on *That Kind of Woman*, blamed the film's failure on Carlo Ponti's interference, asserting, "The best scenes were cut out, and the weak ones were left in and overemphasized by the editing and score." *That Kind of Woman* was shown at the Berlin International Film Festival, Germany, in June 1959. The US premiere was on September 11, 1959 in New York.

---

[99] *The Philadelphia Inquirer*, September 15, 1959.

[100] *The Pittsburgh Press*, September 24, 1959.

That Kind of Woman pre-production photo feauring unknown man, Marcello Girosi, Barbara, unknown man, Sophia Loren and Carlo Ponti.

Barbara taking directions from Sidney Lumet.

Shooting on location. Sophia Loren, Tab Hunter, Barbara and Jack Warden.

Barbara and Sophia Loren are watched by Tab Hunter.

Barbara with Sophia Loren and Keenan Wynn. (Courtesy of Janice Pease).

Barbara with Sophia Loren and Jack Warden. (Courtesy of Janice Pease).

Barbara and Sophia Loren. (Courtesy of Janice Pease).

Barbara with Sophia Loren and Tab Hunter.

Publicity photo for *That Kind of Woman*.

Publicity photo for *That Kind of Woman*.

TV Star and Acclaim

The Sweet Smell of Success and *That Kind of Woman* had shown that Barbara was a talented actress. Nevertheless, she was not picked up for other leading parts by movie producers. She was only signed for one film production starting at the end of the year.

Maybe flirting with television was not appreciated by Hollywood's movie moguls. Being a star in the movies in the early 1950s meant that doing TV was degrading. Although many famous movie actors had blossoming careers on TV at that time the prevailing view was that it was a lesser form of art among actors than being in the movies.

From mid-July to mid-August, Barbara's former lover, Steve Cochran, was shooting *I, Mobster* (1959) in Hollywood. In August, they had several dates. Much to Barbara's dislike, Steve also dated starlet Yvette Vickers, his co-star in *I, Mobster*. Vickers later stated about him, "Steve Cochran was a sweet, funny, loveable rogue, and he was gorgeous, too. But, my God, he drank way too much."[101]

In the fall, when Steve was cast for *The Beat Generation* (1959), their relationship fizzled out. The new movie was filmed in late October and November. Leading lady Mamie Van Doren and Steve also had an affair while filming. Mamie wrote in her autobiography, "Steve Cochran was the rough-hewn, sexy, perennial movie tough guy. What I discovered about Steve after we had been dating for a while was that his behavior was frighteningly erratic. He had a violent temper. In bed, Steve became increasingly rougher until one night he very nearly beat me up. I didn't see him for a while after that—I was plain scared."[102]

Several years later, Barbara spoke with psychic John Cohan about Steve. "Barbara inwardly had a love/hate thing going on with Steve. She was always jealous he had Mamie Van Doren many times over years. Though she did like Mamie a lot, it was a woman thing with her."[103]

Another thing about Steve that had annoyed Barbara was the fact that he was the regular bed mate of Mae West. Mae controlled Cochran like a puppet on a string and had called him several times to "Come up and see me" during the years Barbara was dating him. When a 1957 newspaper mentioned Barbara to be the girl most likely to succeed Mae West, Barbara was to have said that she had no hunkering after her title. "They say I'm a young edition of 'Diamond Lil' and just about everybody is saying I'm taking over on the screen where Mae West left off, but I can't succeed her. She isn't even through

---

[101] www.john-odowd.com

[102] Van Doren, Mamie. *Playing the Field – Sex, Stardom, Love, and Life in Hollywood*. Newport Beach, CA: Starlet Suave Books, 2013.

[103] Source: email contact with author.

yet!" She added, "I'd like to meet her, though. I'd bet we'd have a lot to talk over!"[104]

When Barbara finished working on *That Kind of Woman*, she returned to Hollywood and tried to persuade her parents to move to Los Angeles with her. She didn't succeed. They preferred to stay in their hometown, Huntington, Long Island.

While Barbara was filming in New York, her parents had taken in a young boy to live with them. A 1959 newspaper first mentioned that Barbara had a step-brother, Richard Voorhees. He was born on March 12, 1942. He had an older brother named after their father, Oliver Raymond, who was born in 1898 in Connecticut. He was a war veteran of the Yankee Division, with a war record of previous service in the French army. Due to his experiences in World War II, Oliver was committed to the U.S. Veterans Hospital #108 at Northport, Long Island. He experienced mental problems, and when his wife died, he no longer could take care of his two sons.

Oliver Jr. was able to take care of himself, and later married his sweetheart.

Richard, however, was too young and was "adopted" by Barbara's parents. Janice Pease remembered Richard as a likable guy. He worked for her dad's auto body shop. According to Janice, Barbara and Richard got along fine, as far as she could see. Richard Voorhees died in 1985. His obituary listed George and Julia as his parents.

In the 1970s, George and Julia took in other foster children to live with them. Besides the money aspect of taking in foster children, Barbara's parents also decided to do this because Julia loved children, and with her own daughter grown up and a career woman, she found satisfaction raising a child who needed her support.

Barbara's second cousin, John Carpenter, recalled that both Julia and Ruthie had foster kids. "Julia felt sorry for her foster children and wasn't cruel at all which is fitting with how I recall Julia's personality."[105]

---

[104] *The Daily Review*, March 19, 1957.

[105] Source: email contact with author.

Back in Los Angeles, Barbara resumed her acting career and was cast for two episodes of the popular *The Bob Cummings Show* TV series with Robert Cummings. In September 1958, she was featured in the Fifth Season opening episode, "Bob and Schultzy Reunite." She was cast as ex-waitress Marian Billington, a dumb blonde. When Bob's secretary, Schultzy, leaves Bob to work in a missile factory, Bob hires Marian. He comes to regret this soon, because Marian makes a mess of her job. The following week, Barbara played Marian again in "Bob and the Dumb Blonde."

At the Desilu studios, owned by Lucille Ball and husband Desi Arnaz, Barbara shot the pilot for a possible new comedy series called *All About Abby*, later re-titled as *All About Barbara*. The show would star Barbara as a musical comedy star who gives up her career to marry a small town college professor. The pilot, which was produced by Quinn Martin and written by his wife, Madelyn Pugh Marin, and Bob Carroll, Jr., wasn't sold. In 1963, the CBS television network had bought the pilot and broadcasted it on their Vacation Playhouse program.

In an interview dated April 10, 1958, Barbara mentioned that she was up for a TV series based on the *Maisie* film series that had starred Ann Sothern. "I really like to do that. I'd like it because I'd have to work day and night; and that would be fine for me since I'm not married. The people who work on series work until all hours of the night. I want to have a piece of a series." The *Maisie* series were never made, and with the delayed distribution of her own possible series *All About Abby*, her wish to star in her own TV series seemed unlikely to realize.

After the holiday season, Barbara started working on the drama, *Woman Obsessed*, with Susan Hayward and Stephen Boyd. Filming began in late December 1958, but was then suspended until early January 1959. Barbara plays Mayme, a shop owner in a small town in the wilds of the Canadian Northwest. Susan Hayward plays a widow living on a remote farm with her son. When she hires help, Stephen Boyd, the two fall in love. Because of Boyd's physical abuse of both the boy and his mother, he lands in jail. He then realizes that he's got to change his ways.

Under contract at 20th Century Fox at the time, child actor Dennis Holmes (1950) found the making of the movie a wonderful experience, even though not everyone on the set was that nice to the eight-year-old boy.

Dennis recalled the scene with Barbara and Susan in the town's shop. "I do remember that scene. It was one of the few times that I was actually in a scene with Barbara. She was one of the friendliest actresses I worked with. I'm gathering Susan Hayward didn't like kids. Normally in a production, when you're gonna act with someone, you talk a little bit about your relationship and anything, you know. The first time that I ever spoke to Susan Hayward was when the cameras were rolling. She never even said hello to me, and that was my mom in the movie! Barbara I remember as much sweeter. I didn't really interact with her behind the scenes, but she was around a lot of the scenes we did. I didn't get to know her really well, but I remember her being a very sweet person."

On the set, Barbara got along very well with actor Stephen Boyd. Dennis remembered Boyd as "One of the nicest, kindest, just best people I've ever met in my life. A true gentleman."

He could not say that about the director. "Mr. Hathaway screamed and yelled at me most of the time. He was not a kind man and he was like that with anyone; very dictatorial. But if you did a scene good he was immediately praising you and loving you. So, he was either really mad or really happy." [106]

Reviews were harsh and accused Susan and Stephen of lacklustre performances. Barbara was third billed, but has just a handful of scenes. Most critics left her unmentioned, which probably was a good thing, especially Bosley Crowther of *The New York Times*. He was merciless in his review. "Perhaps we should not blame Miss Hayward or the fellow who plays the husband, Stephen Boyd, for faults that should be laid to the director, Henry Hathaway, or particularly to [script writer] Mr. Boehm. (The latter also produced the picture, so he is liable to double jeopardy.) But their efforts are so clearly indifferent and wanting in basic skill that they are deserving serious censure for such an utterly foolish film."

[106] Source: telephone conversation with author, 4-26-2015.

Again for her wardrobe, 20th Century Fox chose a dress that Marilyn Monroe had worn in one of her movies—the red button-down dress from *Niagara* (1953). With Marilyn away from the studio for two years, and Jayne Mansfield in Great Britain and Spain to film three pictures, the studio used Barbara as a stand-in Marilyn/Jayne-type character.

On March 16, 1959, Barbara returned to the Desilu studios for another pilot show for a new series called *The Untouchables*. Robert Stack played Eliot Ness, a Prohibition Era FBI agent. First televised as a two-part episode of the Westinghouse Desilu Playhouse in April 1959, some episodes of *The Untouchables* were later combined into a feature film titled *The Scarface Mob*.

Barbara, looking radiant, plays Barbara Ritchie, also known as Brandy La France, a Burlesque performer, whose husband, George Ritchie, is a minor gangster. George is also Brandy's fan, and he recommends her act to an acquaintance, who's actually one of Eliot Ness's men. "Go in the afternoon. You'll get seats down the front." To which, Brandy adds, "And come backstage after the show." The number was quite daring for a television show at the time.

Barbara gave a top-notch performance, convincingly playing Brandy as a double-crossing, sweet-talking broad who's using men to better herself. The part where she's infuriated by one of Ness's men who's not biting the bait shows that she was a very talented actress. Her performance won her the *Look* magazine award for Best Performing Actress in a TV Show in 1961.

During filming, Barbara started an affair with the show's producer, Quinn Martin, who was unhappy in his marriage. Originally a writer for television shows, Martin had the ambition of becoming a producer, but his wife, Madelyn Pugh Martin, was none too supportive. His affair with Barbara was the final straw and resulted in their divorce.

Their relationship lasted for a couple of months. Barbara found it frustrating that Madelyn manipulated him with his son, Michael, and she broke up with Martin because his ex-wife called too often with so-called emergencies, usually involving Michael. In 1961, he married Marianne Webb.

Burlesque dancer Rusty Lane was hired to show Barbara the art of stripping. Because Barbara played a stripper many times in her career, she didn't need much help in learning the ropes. Miss Lane remembered, "Barbara showed a talent for genteel peeling. She shocked me. I thought I would have to spend a couple of weeks teaching her the ropes, but in one day she had the whole routine down pat. Too pat." Lane continued, "She was so good that we were afraid she might be overdoing it. So, she decided to give a preview performance for the producer and the cast. Bob Stack, Keenan Wynn, Neville, and Pat Crowley were in the audience. They almost fainted when Barbara went into her act. Right away, the producer called in a dance director to modify her number, so it wouldn't burn out TV tubes all over the country."[107]

Barbara commented to a reporter who interviewed her on the set. "Honey, I've played so many strippers, sometimes I feel like one. You can do side bumps on TV, but you can't do front bumps. Rusty didn't know that. Then, she wanted me to sing 'Honeysuckle Rose.' I heard that and I know I'm dead already. We changed it to 'Ain't Misbehavin' and I play against the sex, see? Then, we shoot my face close up. You know I'm grinding away down below, but I figure you can get a lot of sex in the face. What d'ya think?" Barbara's strip scene took six hours to shoot.

Chuck Landis, owner of the popular Hollywood *Club Largo,* also took notice and offered Barbara a mere $1,500 a week if she would strip in his club. Barbara answered that she earned more with stripping on the screen than in person. Besides, she remarked, "I want to get married. I want to have lots of children, and I don't want to tell them that I knocked them dead on the runway at Minsky's."[108]

Desilu offered Barbara another contract to appear in the popular comedy series, *The Real McCoys.* In "The Politician," she plays Gladys, the not too bright wife of politician Jim Slade. Robert Middleton plays a dishonest candidate for the United States House of Representatives, who falsely claims

---

[107] *Inside Story,* July 1961.
[108] *The Lowdown,* May 1960.

to have previously been a farmer in a bid for the farm vote. Unintentionally Gladys is part of her husband's unmasking.

Barbara was extremely funny in yet another part as a not-so-bright blonde bimbo. She was very proud of this appearance. "It's one of these 'Born Yesterday' stories. This politician was once a garbage collector and he's upgraded himself to a big wheel in political circles. I play his wife—and get loaded."

Barbara's parts and comedy timing didn't stay unnoticed, and famous TV comedians were soon lining up to sign her for their shows.

A notable television appearance was on the *Jack Benny Program*, which aired on November 15, 1959. Special guest stars are actor James Stewart and his wife, Gloria. Jack explains to his audience that the couple begged him to come to their anniversary party. However, Stewart explains to his wife that he couldn't stop Jack from inviting himself.

Barbara plays Benny's girlfriend, Mildred Meyerhouser. In answer to her husband's apologies, Gloria says, "I don't mind Jack so much, but those girls he always brings with him. I wonder what kind of girl he brings this time?" And in comes Mildred, a CBS telephone operator, and proud of it! Mildred is a loud-mouthed, outspoken dumb blonde.

Later that evening, Mildred is dancing with James Stewart. "Whoever thought that I, Mildred Meyerhouser, would someday be dancing with a real movie star?" When Stewart makes a remark about her unusual name, she answers, "I thought about changing it, but somebody said when you change your name, sometimes it changes your whole personality."

"And you did not take the gamble?" Stewart remarks.

To which, Barbara looks shocked.

Later, when Barbara belts out her favorite song, "La Vie en Rose," the whole club gasps at Mildred and a very uncomfortable Stewart. This sketch proved again that she had perfect comedic timing.

Barbara told *TV Guide* in 1960 how she got the part on *The Jack Benny Program*. "I was working with Red [Skelton] on a *Shower of Stars* a couple of years ago. Seymour Berns, the director, asked me if I'd like to play Jack

Benny's girlfriend. He was directing Benny, too. I said, 'Sure, who wouldn't?' Just about that time, I had to kiss Red—in the scene, I mean. Lynn Bari was supposed to discover Red kissing me and hit him over the head with a rubber shovel. She hit him so hard he bit my lip. The lip began to bleed, then it began to swell. They had to get ice and then a nurse. Well, it was a mess. Lynn said she was sorry. She didn't mean to, I don't think.

"So, that's how I was with a swollen lip when Jack interviewed me the next day. Jack said, 'Gee, Barbara, you're too young to play my girlfriend.' I looked him in the eye and said, 'Jack, you don't know some of the men I go out with!' I got the part."[109]

About working with Barbara, Jack Benny commented, "I spotted her immediately. I liked her delivery. She's very talented, very interesting, looks good, and is just right for my show. A good actress."

The character of Mildred Meyerhouser became a semi-regular on Benny's program. Barbara played the dumb blonde four times in total. She seemed to have become the personification of Mildred a couple of years later, when newspaper articles and movie magazines mentioned Barbara's love of alcoholic beverages and her loud behavior when dining out.

Earl Wilson reported in August 1961, "Caesar Romero and Barbara Nichols, the world's loudest laughter, dined at Luchow's and then hit the Latin Quarter, where Barbara out laughed even Jack Durant."

On January 7, 1962, Wilson described Barbara's "... famous laugh, which shakes pictures off walls, ricocheted through the Cordial restaurant."

Actress Gloria Pall remembered a similar event. "One night in the 1960s, I was at a celebrity-filled restaurant in Beverly Hills called La Scala with a VIP producer. Who is sitting across the room from us? You know who, Miss Miserable herself. She was wedged between her escorts, giggling out loud and apparently high as a kite. She kept slipping under the table and they kept pulling her back up. I guess she was used to working under the table!"[110]

---

[109] *TV Guide*, July 23-29, 1960.

[110] Source: email contact with author.

Barbara in TV's *All About Barbara*, 1958.

Barbara with Susan Hayward and Dennis Holmes in *Woman Obsessed*, 1959.

Barbara and Stephen Boyd on the set of *Woman Obsessed*, 1959.

Barbara and Theodore Bikel in *Woman Obsessed*, 1959.

Pubicity photo for *The Untouchables*, 1959.

Barbara's striptease in *The Untouchables*, 1959.

TV Star and Acclaim

Barbara and Robert Stack in the episode "The Empty Chair" of TV's *The Untouchables*, 1959.

Barbara with Jack Benny, James and Gloria Stewart on *The Jack Benny Program*, 1959.

MGM publicity photo, 1960.

Who Was That Lady?

THE COMEDY, *WHO WAS THAT LADY?* (1960), reunited Barbara with fellow blonde actress Joi Lansing. Back in 1953, when they were modeling for Bernard of Hollywood, both girls were invited to have dinner with Clark Gable and the photographer. Apart from the dinner, there's no account of what happened that night! Besides meeting each other at several Hollywood parties, the two women were part of a photo shoot for *TV Guide* together as a part of promoting the new season of *Maverick*, in which they both appeared, prior to shooting *Who Was That Lady?*

Who Was That Lady? starred Janet Leigh, Tony Curtis, and Dean Martin.

Janet and Tony were having serious marital problems during filming. It was to be their last movie together. Nevertheless, as Janet Leigh reminisced in her 1984 autobiography, it was a happy set. "We really rolled with this one. The personal familiarity of the three of us allowed absolute freedom, and the interplay was wild and woolly and inventive. There was an atmosphere of playfulness on the set that lent itself to practical jokes, attempts to make each other laugh in the middle of takes, and escalating water fights."

According to a July 1958 *Los Angeles Examiner* news item, Bob Hope and Bing Crosby were interested in starring in the film version of Norman Krasna's play. The same newspaper noted in March 1959 that Debbie Reynolds was to co-star in the film.

In November 1959, another newspaper stated that a six-week search for two blondes, further described as "sexpot entertainers," had ended with the selection of Joi and Barbara. That makes the scene with them probably one of the last scenes shot for this production. It was filmed between July 20 and August 25, 1959, and additional scenes were filmed late 1959. The film premiered on April 15, 1960.

The story is about an Assistant-Professor of Chemistry at Columbia University (Tony Curtis). While he is kissing a student, he is caught in the act by his wife, and she then wants to divorce him. Dean Martin, a writer for TV shows, helps his buddy out by thinking out a scenario that makes the two men FBI agents. Tony first detests the idea, but Dean makes him believe that he truly is a FBI man. Quickly after he concludes that if he falls for his lies, his wife surely will believe their scheme. They arrange the props needed; a FBI identification card for Tony is made.

At first, Janet doesn't fall for Tony's story and threatens to throw him out. When she sees the ID card, she's baffled and begs for forgiveness. Because the FBI ID card wasn't used for a TV program, the prop man notifies the FBI about the fraud. Federal Agent Powell pays Ann a visit and he soon finds out what's going on.

Dean picks up Tony for an assignment, much to his disagreement. Tony, being the wiser one, wants to stop the charade, but Dean makes it worse by the minute, dishing up a story about two foreign spies they have to unmask.

Dean says, "I've got two sensational dames. They're a sister act. They won't separate. They'll separate when they've got enough liquor in them."

To which, Tony replies that he is happily married, and he doesn't want any outside women.

Fifty-four minutes into the movie, Barbara and Joi appear—and what kind of appearance! They are greeted by the doorman of Wong's restaurant, and, before the girls walk in, they bend over to adjust their stockings. "Get a load of how these girls are assembled," Dean tells Tony. After their jaw-dropping entrance, the girls join the boys in their booth. Barbara wants to eat a cookie, but suddenly stops, exclaiming, "I have to be careful what I swallow today."

Dean claims that Tony is vice president for CBS, "and that he uses girls", as Dean likes to add. The meeting with the girls becomes sort of an interview for them to land a part in a TV show.

"You do use girls, don't you?" Dean asks Tony.

Barbara remarks, "He thought you might use us."

Dean replies, "I couldn't put it better myself."

Joi adds, "We're very versatile. We sing and dance."

Who Was That Lady? reached #17 at the box office for 1960, grossing over $3 million. The *Motion Picture Herald* reported about Barbara and Joi's appearance. "Barbara Nichols and Joi Lansing play a typically narrow-minded but broadly-built pair of sisters [Dean] Martin is trying to seduce."

The New York Times also mentioned Joi and Barbara. "It gets even funnier when, with Miss Leigh braced for sacrifices 'in line of F.B.I. duty,' Mr. Martin drags her nervous spouse out on a double-date with two palpitating showgirls, Barbara Nichols and Joi Lansing."

Actress Dyanne Thorne (1943) made her movie debut in *Who Was That Lady?* She remembered, "At the time, I was taking classes at New York University and was looking to make my mark and get started. I was working, as they call it, as an extra. I was working in a scene that was Janet Leigh's scene. Tony Curtis and Janet Leigh worked the day that I worked. I didn't get to meet Barbara and Joi on that movie, but the rumors on the set were that both these ladies were very easy to work with and just everybody loved their personalities. Their colleagues thought the world of them."[111]

On December 8, the best-edited theatrical and television films of 1959 were honored at a cocktail party in the Crystal Room of the Beverly Hills Hotel. Among the actors presenting the honors were David Niven, Eva Marie Saint, John Cassavetes, Peggie Castle, and Barbara.

In 1959, Barbara decided to join a health club and worked out on a regular basis: "I feel so much better since I've joined a health club. When I'm not doing a picture, I try to have a workout in the gym every day, and I enjoy the relaxation a steam room gives me. I grew up in New York in an Italian neighborhood, and I love Italian food. But since I came to Hollywood I don't eat it very often. I have to count my calories. After seeing my first screen test, I began to reduce. I went on a severe diet of 750 calories until I got the size I wanted to be. And to stay that way, I've cut out bread and butter, potatoes, most fried things, and soft drinks. But there's no doubt about it, you can eat more without gaining if you exercise."[112]

Actress Gloria Pall, not a fan of Barbara, ran into her at the gym. "In the early 1960s, I joined the Beverly Hills health club, and one day, she was leaving as I was entering. Again, I greeted her, and again, she ignored me. Then, I said, 'You have a serious problem,' which she also ignored. She was from Queens. Well, she certainly was a Queen—that is Queen of the Bitches and Miserables!"[113]

Barbara also took swimming lessons at the Health Club. A part in a new movie required that she film a scene in a fish tank. She told a reporter at the

---

[111] Source: telephone conversation with author, 3-20-2015.

[112] *Sarasota Herald-Tribune,* June 3, 1959.

[113] Source: email contact with author.

time, "You know, honey, I almost drowned in the ocean when I was a little girl and have been afraid of the water ever since."[114]

Barbara's new healthy look was greatly showed off in her new picture, *Where the Boys Are* (1960). The picture was shot on the MGM soundstage and on location in Fort Lauderdale, Florida between June 23 and September 1960.

The simple story involves four student girlfriends, who enjoy their spring break and meet some boys. Barbara plays Lola Fandango, The Sea Nymph of the Tropical Isle," and an artiste like Esther Williams. Lola entertains customers of a restaurant, doing a water ballet act in a huge water basin. Lola also sings "Have You Met Miss Fandango?" on the beach in a tight pink dress.

On her swim scene, Barbara commented, "The director keeps asking me to smile underwater. I got enough trouble to keep from drowning and he wants a smile."

Barbara got a private lifeguard for the scene. "He's even on the bottom of the pool waiting for me when I go under water. I want him close by because in another scene I have to get popped out of a giant clamshell. My main problem, though, is that I'm too buoyant and can't stay on the bottom of the pool. They wanted to put weights inside my bathing suit, but it's too tight. My trainer says I'm so buoyant that I couldn't drown if I tried. But, that's what he thinks."[115]

This particular scene took three days to shoot with the main characters spending four hours a day underwater.

Connie Francis, making her motion picture debut as an actress, sings the title song, as well as "Turn on the Sunshine." Barbara told John Cohan that she seduced Connie Francis, which led to an affair. She was so elated telling Cohan about her conquest.

Cohan said, "Barbara said to me, 'Connie has great sauce and I'm not talking Pasta honey.'"[116]

---

[114] *Sunday Herald*, August 7, 1960.

[115] *Sunday Herald*, August 7, 1960.

[116] Source: email contact with author.

One of her last assignments in 1960 reunited Barbara with former colleagues George Sanders and Cliff Robertson. The General Electric TV episode, "The Small Elephants," was shot at Universal Studios. Actor Marvin Kaplan (1927) played a small part in the series. Kaplan remembered, "I knew Barbara fairly well. She wasn't just the chorine. She could be a moving serious actress, but she was a sad lady. George Sanders was also a quiet, sad man."

Kaplan recalled that he, Barbara, and the rest of the cast were sitting in the commissary when she tried to attract the attention of Richard Widmark by lifting her stockinged leg into the air. Widmark was filming *Judgement at Nuremberg* at Universal. "Widmark was amused but horrified. We all wanted to be at another table, but that was Barbara. You couldn't help but like her. She didn't respect herself or her talent. I think she thought that people only wanted her body, that no one loved her or took her acting talent seriously. She was heart-breaking in her scene with Tony Curtis in *Sweet Smell of Success*. Lots of wonderful actresses who played bimbos, like Iris Adrian, had long and fulfilling careers, but they were better balanced than Barbara."[117]

In February 1961, Barbara starred in an unsold pilot for a proposed sitcom about an airline hostess called *Coffee, Tea, or Milk*, produced by Jack Webb. "At a time when very sexy (and busty) women were not a prominent part of TV series, an attempt was made to change that image with Barbara playing a Marilyn Monroe-like stewardess, whose comical adventures in the various cities she visits would provide the basis for each episode."[118]

A Season 2 episode of *The Twilight Zone*, "Twenty-Two," featured her in a leading role that was broadcast nationwide in February that year. Rod Serling's opening narration went, "This is Miss Liz Powell. She's a professional dancer and she's in the hospital as a result of overwork and nervous fatigue. And at this moment, we have just finished walking with her in a nightmare. In a moment, she'll wake up and we'll remain at her side. The problem here is that both Miss Powell and you will reach a point where it might be difficult

---

[117] Source: email contact with author.
[118] Terrace, Vincent. *Encyclopedia of Television Pilots 1937-2012*. Jefferson: McFarland & Company, Inc., 2013.

to decide which is reality and which is nightmare, a problem uncommon perhaps but rather peculiar to the Twilight Zone."

Liz keeps dreaming that a nurse takes her to room 22, which turns out to be the hospital morgue. She tells her doctor about her dreams. He comforts her and blames it on her burnout. When she is allowed to leave, the mysterious nurse from her dreams reappears as a stewardess, when Liz is about to take flight 22 to Miami.

Barbara again shows her acting skills to full advantage, playing the frightened and confused Miss Liz Powell. She received much acclaim from critics and TV viewers, and today the episode is considered as one of the series best.

Filming the hospital scenes, Barbara showed up on set in full make-up with a gorgeous nightgown. She was a little disappointed, when director Jack Smight told her she would be wearing a hospital gown and less make-up. Eventually, he gave in to her, who was allowed to wear the clothes she had chosen originally. In the other scene, where she runs out of the plane and down the boarding steps, she loses her footing, but she catches herself and keeps going, never breaking character. Director Smight loved it and kept that accident in the final print.

On March 2nd, 1961, while Barbara was nightclubbing at the Pink Pussycat at Santa Monica Boulevard, an unpleasant event took place at her home. Burglars forced through a window to gain entry and stole furs and jewellery worth between $3,000 and $5,000. In October, after months of police investigation, five men and two women were jailed on suspicion of burglarizing the home. The two women—Martha "Georgia Raft" Pariseau and Sylvia "Peeler Lawford" Williams—were dancers at the Pink Pussycat night club. One of the men arrested, Robert L. Edwards, formerly worked as a bartender at the night spot. He'd tipped the others that Barbara was at the nightclub at the night of the robbery.

Barbara and Joi Lansing, *Who Was That Lady*, 1960.

Barbara with Tony Curtis, Joi Lansing and Dean Martin in *Who Was That Lady*, 1960.

Barbara with Janet Leigh and Joi Lansing in *Who Was That Lady*, 1960.

Publicity photo for *Where the Boys Are*, 1960.

Barbara and Jim Hutton in *Where the Boys Are*, 1960.

Barbara, Jim Hutton, Paula Prentiss, Dolores Hart, George Hamilton, Connie Francis and Frank Gorshin in *Where the Boys Are*, 1960.

MGM publicity photo, 1960.

Barbara and George Sanders in TV's *The Small Elephants*, 1961.

Barbara and Fredd Wayne in the episode "Twenty Two" of TV's *The Twilight Zone*, 1961.

Women in Love

OVER THE YEARS, BARBARA HAD INDULGED in sexual affairs with both men and women. After her fling with Connie Francis, she had an affair with actress Barbara Stanwyck. The affair with Stanwyck was on and off during the 1960s. According to John Cohan, Stanwyck promised Barbara meaty roles in her future, but never came through on that promise. Cohan also claimed that Barbara and Marilyn Monroe got real close. "From what I recall of Barbara talking on Marilyn Monroe, professionally, she admired what Marilyn accomplished, considering what she had to offer as an actress, but personally, they both had a big fight after a lesbian sleepover. Because of that, Barbara was still angry with Marilyn. I recall Barbara saying it was after she did *Where the Boys Are*, for Marilyn was asking her about Connie Francis. She liked Connie's song from the movie, among other things! Marilyn definitely burned the candle on both ends. She bedded Jeanne Carmen, Shelley Winters, Lili St. Cyr, to name just a few."[119]

Barbara discussed the matter of marriage and relationships with John Cohan regularly. Cohan said, "As far as men and lasting relationships, Barbara said she never found that kind of happiness with any of them, and she certainly gave it her all and tried."[120]

Barbara once commented, "Too many men I meet socially confuse me with the types I've played. Married men never introduce me to their wives and women. Even those I've known for years seldom introduce me to their boyfriends or husbands." She added, "Just a little while ago, for instance, a girl I know got married. I used to see her all the time, but all of a sudden she started avoiding me like I had the plague or something. I couldn't understand why, until I heard she was engaged. Then I knew she was afraid I'd try to steal her guy."[121]

As with her dates with men, Barbara had not yet met a woman who truly set her heart on fire, but that would change within the year.

Back in the Hollywood movie studios, she started filming the prison drama, *House of Women* (1962). Announced in the March 16, 1961 edition of *Variety* as *Ladies of the Mob*, filming started in mid-May 1961 at Warner Bros. Burbank Studios.

Ten days into the shooting, Walter Doniger, who had been initially hired to direct the film, was fired and replaced by the movie's scriptwriter, Crane Wilbur. Shirley Knight (1936), the movie's leading actress and a promising young contract player at Warner Bros. at the time, remembered, "The change of director was horrible. There was no reason, and the replacement was awful. Also, there was a girlfriend of his, who couldn't open the prison gate on cue,

---

[119] Source: email contact with author.
[120] Source: email contact with author.
[121] *Inside Story*, July 1961.

and it was an emotional scene, where I had to try to run through the gate and grab my daughter. The girlfriend kept ruining the shot until I had to insist she be replaced. Barbara was very sweet and kind to me. She took care of me when the dreadful man took the director's place."[122]

The story concerns an inmate called Erica (Shirley Knight), a pregnant woman, who is wrongly implicated in a crime and sent to prison for five years. Giving birth to her baby in prison, Erica hopes to get parole so she can raise the child in a proper atmosphere. Things get tough, when the warden Cole falls in love with her and doesn't want her to get paroled. When Erica's daughter is given up for adoption without her consent, the inmates revolt against the wardens.

Barbara was cast as Candy Kane, an ex-stripper. In and out of prison since the age of eleven, Candy declines her parole, stating she will never be able to adjust to the outside world.

At times, Barbara's acting is strong and, as usual, she's very funny in most of her scenes with the other inmates. She received a positive review in *The New York Times*. "The brightest things in this melodramatic pottage are Miss Nichols, as a saucy ex-strip teaser, and Virginia Gregg, a consistently good bit player, as a parole board member."

Knight remembered Barbara fondly. "We became friends on that film. She was a terrific woman. I adored her. She was funny and helped me a lot, as I was angry that I was put in a B-film after my Oscar nomination. Although I did not know her well, I enjoyed her company and she always made me laugh."[123]

Knight was nominated for the Academy Award and the Golden Globe for her part in *The Dark at the Top of the Stairs* (1960) and was also nominated for those same awards for *Sweet Bird of Youth* (1962).

In the script of *House of Women*, the inmates drool over a picture of their favorite pin-up boy. A prop man presumptuously tacked a photo of Marlon

---

[122] Source: email contact with author.

[123] Source: email contact with author.

Brando on the prison wall, but Barbara, Shirley Knight, and Constance Ford conducted a poll among the other actresses and demanded a change. The Brando picture was changed with one of Edd Byrnes, the TV actor. However, the final print of the movie doesn't show Byrnes, but Warner Bros.' contract player, Troy Donahue, as the heartthrob two inmates are arguing over.

During an outdoor scene in the prison yard, Troy's name has clearly been dubbed over the women saying Byrnes' name, suggesting the exterior was shot first and the decision to use Troy's name was a later idea integrated during interior shooting. Troy had visited the actresses on the set during filming.

Character actress Constance Ford plays the part of the leader of the prison riot. Barbara and Constance became lovers during the filming. Their relationship lasted several months. Barbara later told John Cohan that Constance and she were in "heaven" during their love affair. Although Constance became very controlling, Barbara named her top of her list as her "soul mate."

During filming, neither Shirley Knight nor the rest of the crew were aware of the relationship. Shirley remembered, "I would not have been aware of it, as I wouldn't at that time of my life even known what it meant. I was a young girl from Kansas, and had never even known about two males or two females being lovers."

Constance Ford (1923-1993) was born in The Bronx, New York. She initially worked as a model, and her face became famous in an Elizabeth Arden advertising campaign in 1941. She studied acting and appeared on television from 1949, the year she also made her debut on Broadway. In the 1960s, she appeared in a couple of movies, and during her relationship with Barbara, she played in several TV series. After shooting *House of Women* had commenced, Barbara and Constance spent as much time together as their busy work schedules allowed.

While working on *House of Women*, Barbara was asked to be one of the celebrity readers on the children's hour on radio station KPFK. She read a couple of chapters of the book, *Tom Swift and his Electric Motorcycle*. About working on radio, she commented, "I hate radio. I have claustrophobia and I can't stand the dingy, little studios where you have to perform without an audience."[124]

For her next production, Barbara was cast to portray real life entertainer Texas Guinan in *The George Raft Story* (1961). Filming started in August 1961 on the Warner Bros. lot. Crane Wilbur, who replaced the director in *House of Women*, had also written the script for *The George Raft Story*.

On August 4, George Raft visited the set when Barbara shot her scenes. Julie London, Barrie Chase, Margo Moore, and Jayne Mansfield participated in a photo shoot with George that day. Barbara did not take part in the photo shoot with her female co-stars, but after shooting her scene, she was photographed with George and Jayne. Barbara and George were old friends; the two had met occasionally from the late fifties on. George also secured Barbara a part in his biopic. He was paid $25,000 for his story and a fat percentage of the picture's profits. He was portrayed by Ray Danton.

Barbara had three costume changes in her mere five minutes of screen time. Dressed in Marilyn Monroe's dress from *Some Like it Hot* (1959), Texas greeted her audience with the raucous cry, "Hello suckers! How's the mob treating you?" before giving away a performance, singing "I Never Knew I Could Love Anybody" and "You've Got to See Mama Every Night."[125]

Barbara fitted the part of the roaring twenties' gang moll/entertainer perfectly. Texas was a small part, but so were all the female parts in *The George Raft Story*.

Variety wrote in its review, "Five women are shown involved in Raft's life—each a shallow, shadowy, inconclusive interlude. They are played by Jayne Mansfield, Julie London, Barrie Chase, Barbara Nichols, and Margo Moore. Their roles enable Jayne Mansfield to display her astonishing physique, Miss London to croon a sultry vocal, Miss Chase to showcase her hoofing prowess, Miss Nichols to render a flashy song-and-dance as Texas Guinan, and Miss

---

[124] *Los Angeles Mirror*, June 7, 1961.

[125] Barbara's voice was dubbed.

Moore to snare histrionic honors from the other members of this good-looking quintet."[126]

The press had a wild time guessing which actress portrayed which of George's real-life former lovers. Texas is the only exception. George commented, "I don't know who's playing who. The truth of the matter is that this movie is semi-fictional. Parts of it are true, and parts of it are fiction. The parts concerning the dames are fictional. They've got to be for two reasons: one, I'm not the kind of guy who kisses and tells, no matter how much the dough; and two, if we were going to use real identifiable people, we'd have to pay them clearance fees for invading their privacy, and those dames would probably want millions."

The George Raft Story premiered in Chicago on November 22, 1961. Dancer and actor Christopher Riordan recalled a memory of his friend, actress Barrie Chase, who worked with Barbara in *Pal Joey* and *The George Raft Story*. "A friend of mine worked with her a couple of times, and said she felt sorry for Barbara. She wasn't really dumb, but she was always distracted. Something else was seemingly taking up her thought process."[127]

In a 1956 interview in *Modern Man* magazine, Barbara described herself as a person who tends to be nervous. In a 1957 TV interview, she added to her nervousness that she disliked crowds and phonies. "First of all, I get kind of claustrophobic in the middle of everything, like crowds. And phonies I dislike intensely. Anyone who is not sincere. I think you meet some in all walks of life not only in Hollywood."[128]

Two years later, Barbara commented on career uncertainties and the competitive life in Hollywood. "If you're to avoid ulcers and sleeping pills, you have to learn to laugh at yourself. Thank heaven I have a sense of humor. I don't brood, feel sorry for myself, or look back. I try to believe that something really wonderful may happen. But I'm inclined to be nervous."[129]

---

[126] *Variety*, December 6, 1961.

[127] Source: email contact with author.

[128] *TV's Tabloid*, July 3, 1957.

[129] *Sarasota Herald-Tribune*, June 3, 1959.

Janice Pease, Barbara's cousin remembered that Barbara took Constance Ford to her parent's house in the summer of 1961. "She was friends with Connie Ford. She came to our home with Barbara when she was in rehearsals for *Let It Ride!* They had a falling out after years as best female friends. I remember getting Connie's autograph and that she and Barbara were close. I know Barbara stayed with us a few days. I don't think Connie did, but she was at our house the day of the show. She was nice."[130]

In winter 1961, Constance started filming *Roman Adventure* (1962) with Troy Donahue and Suzanne Pleshette. John Cohan recalled, "Barbara said Suzanne Pleshette was one of the causes for the breakup. Suzanne was bisexual. Barbara told me often how upset she was with Suzanne Pleshette, because she always felt Connie Ford, her then lover, could have made a long-term relationship. Though Suzanne became a movie star in 1962, Connie Ford knew Suzanne from the New York City days. Barbara and Suzanne actually had a real catfight when all the drama was going on with Connie and her. Suzanne had broken a tooth of Barbara's and gave her a bloody nose. Barbara said she gave Suzanne a black eye and a pulled out big stands of her hair. When Barbara saw Suzanne in later years when Suzanne was very famous, Barbara yelled out in crowded restaurants 'Oh, there's Suzanne Pleshette that butch dyke over there!' They always hated each other till their demise. Barbara would say, when Suzanne and Troy Donahue married for a very short time, 'Suzanne's voice is deeper than Troy's, and Troy's hair is longer than Suzanne's. You know who the bottom in that relationship is.' Troy Donahue was gay, but would have what he called 'mercy lays' with women."[131]

Barbara was devastated after ending her relationship with Constance. She was very depressed and had a hard time adjusting to a life on her own again. As always in her dark times, her alcohol use intensified.

---

[130] Source: email contact with author.

[131] Source: email contact with author.

Barbara and Shirley Knight taking directions from Walter Doniger, *House of Women*, 1962.

Barbara, Shirley Knight and Constance Ford in *House of Women*, 1962.

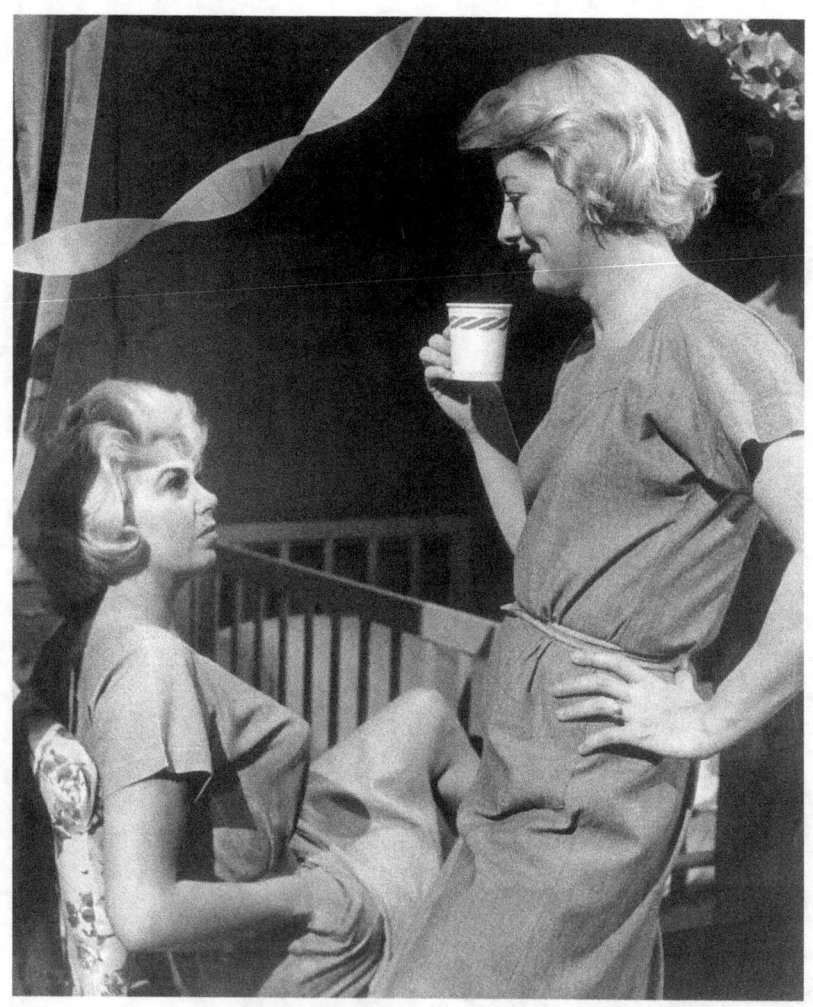
Barbara and Constance Ford on the set of *House of Women*, 1962. (Courtesy of Janice Pease).

House of Women, 1962.

Barbara and George Raft.

Barbara and Ray Danton on the set of *The George Raft Story*, 1961.

Barbara in *The George Raft Story*, 1961.

Barbara at her parents home, December 1961.

Losing Grip

BARBARA WAS BACK ON BROADWAY when she starred with George Gobel, Paula Stewart, and Sam Levene in the musical comedy, *Let It Ride!* There had been a frantic search for the female lead. Betty Grable, Jayne Mansfield, Diana Dors, Edie Adams, Shelley Winters, and Marilyn Maxwell were all considered. Actress Marie McDonald also wanted the part and she even offered to invest a large sum of money in the production. Gobel had invested a large sum of his own money, and he wanted Betty Grable to play the role that Barbara eventually got to play. Newspapers mention that even as late as June, Betty was reading the script and had to decide if she wanted the role. Even Lauren Bacall was said to have approached Gobel, but in July, the press mentioned that "they settled on Barbara Nichols for a femme lead."[132]

---

[132] *Chicago Daily Tribune*, July 11, 1961.

Rehearsals started in mid-August, and tryouts were held in September 1961 in Philadelphia, Pennsylvania, at the Erlanger Theatre. When the play received negative reviews, playwright Ronny Graham was taken aboard to revise the script.

The play ran from October 12 until December 9 at the Eugene O'Neill Theatre in New York for 68 performances. *Let It Ride!* was not a hit.

Most of the critics were harsh. Howard Taubman in *The New York Times* wrote, "Unhappily, Mr. Gobel rarely ceased to be Mr. Gobel... the songs were only serviceable, and the principals could not sing."

Nevertheless, several reviewers were raving about the show and Barbara. "A bright and entertaining show. Sam Levene can do anything, and do it well; Barbara Nichols is a doll and first class comedienne," and "Barbara Nichols has a shape that will make your eyes bulge!" Barbara sang one song, "I Wouldn't Have Had To," which was also recorded for the Original Cast Album.

Television and nightclub comic George Gobel made his stage debut in *Let It Ride!* He was insecure about his performance because critics noted that he relied heavily on the floor mikes to project throughout the house.

Barbara wasn't very happy in her role of Mabel, either. Once again, she was to portray a stripper. She felt miserable and was left with a broken heart, because there were troubles in her relationship with Constance. Unaware of her vulnerability, George demanded too much from her, and, according to what John Cohan remembered Barbara telling him, also came on to her many times. There was a lot of tension between the two.

However, Paula Stewart denies this. "Gobel came on to her? Very unlikely. He was extremely shy and his wife was always hovering over him. Probably Barbara felt snubbed and took it wrong. He was so low-key, he almost faded into the scenery. As for the show, I hated it. Music was pedestrian and script was equally so. I was glad when it closed."[133]

One evening, Barbara drank a few too many martinis, causing her to fall

---

[133] Source: email contact with author.

off the stage and hurt her leg and shoulder. She had to undergo treatment, and x-rays were taken, revealing she had an extra rib!

Being a real pro, she quickly resumed her performances. In an interview with Earl Wilson, she made fun of the accident. "I owe my doctor so much. I better marry him. Between virus shots and vitamin shots, he saw more of me than anybody."

Her drinking also caused her to be late for rehearsals and performances several times. So, the producer rented a limousine and driver to pick her up for work.

Paula Stewart (1929), who had previously appeared in the successful Broadway show, *Wildcat*, with Lucille Ball, remembered Barbara's agony differently. "She was a complicated person. Beautiful but very vulnerable. Probably the source of her humor. I met her at the first day of rehearsals. My impression was she was uncomfortable with being on stage. Not her medium of choice. She played a 'dingy, blonde, big-busted broad.' I loved George Gobel and all the cast. Barbara had a drinking problem even then and couldn't remember her lines. I always felt sorry for her. She seemed remote and put upon by the others. The producers approached me to take over her part in the show. Now, I was the typical ingénue, and playing her type was, for me, a challenge I would relish! But being less of an opportunist and more insightful, on the train to the out of town try-outs, I sat with her and talked 'turkey', something like, 'Listen honey you're going to be axed if you don't shape up' and 'Show them you can do this part.'

"She really was impressed with my candor and my offer to coach her, which I did, and consequently, she kept the role. After that, we became good buddies. I even introduced her to my ex-husband, Burt Bacharach, who had a fondness for big boobs. I did them both a good turn."

"After the show closed, she went back to Los Angeles. We remained in touch. She had affairs with several big male stars, and I knew she also liked girls, although that was never an issue with us. She respected my preferences. My best friend was Lucille Ball, who was unhappy with my moving next door to Barbara, when I left my then husband, Jack Carter [in 1970]. Lucy suspected Barbara had slept with her former husband, Desi, which Barb denied."[134]

Barbara's eight-year-old cousin, Janice, was very disappointed that she couldn't go to see the show. "I was told I was too young and the show was too risqué. Barbara went back and forth from the theatre to our house in Dix Hills. She used to stay at our house when she was on the Island. I watched her get ready to drive into the city to do *Let It Ride!* on stage. She lit a cigarette. I knew she wasn't a smoker. When I asked her what she was doing, she said she only smoked when she was nervous. I watched her in awe as she applied her make-up and got ready." [135]

Like many of her blonde contemporaries, Barbara, too, experienced a difficult time in 1962. The blonde bombshell type was not much in demand anymore. The little work that was there had to be divided by the remaining actresses who had made a career out of playing dumb blondes.

Barbara was not signed to do any movie work. She only appeared on a couple of game shows and talk shows on television. Together with Mamie Van Doren and Angie Dickinson, she appeared on the TV show *The Dick Powell Theatre* in April. In the episode, "No Strings Attached," Dick appeared as a lawyer, who has to decide between his high-class girlfriend, (Dickinson), and a burlesque stripper client that he's just acquired (Van Doren). The latter is upset that rival, Barbara, has stolen her act, which consists of dressing up like a sexy missile, and with each hip swivel, firing off explosive blasts.

Mamie Van Doren recalled that she, Angie Dickinson, and Barbara got along very well. Van Doren said, "[On the set] Barbara was full of fun and pizzazz. I adored working with her."

On Barbara's fun-loving nature, partying, and people saying that she drank too much, resulting in her getting loud and vulgar, Mamie Van Doren said, "People that say that about her have no sense of humor. She was a

---

[134] Source: email contact with author.

[135] Source: email contact with author.

riot, and I loved being around her. She made me laugh all the time. All my memories of Barbara are good ones. Not a bad bone in her body."[136]

In May, Zsa Zsa Gabor, Kathy Nolan, and Barbara were the mystery guests of *Your First Impression*, a game show that had a panel guess the identity of the mystery guests by throwing questions or sentences at them to finish instantly. Barbara finished the sentence, "If a man gave me a mink coat," with "I'd take it!"

August 5, 1962 newspaper headlines announced the death of Marilyn Monroe. Barbara had known of Monroe's affair with President Kennedy and his brother, Robert. Like her and other actresses, Barbara had also bedded Robert.

John Cohan, later said, "After Marilyn's murder, Barbara said she knew it would happen, for Monroe had a way of stepping on the boys' toes intentionally. That was a no-no. Barbara said she had Bobby Kennedy many times and he was overrated. He behaved like a teenage boy having sex. He was very immature."[137]

On November 19, Barbara was a guest in *Stump the Stars*, the pantomime quiz show that was hosted by Pat Harrington Jr. Besides Barbara, legendary actress Hedy Lamarr was one of the show's guest stars. The show requested the contestants to be themselves and to think on their feet without a script.

Beverly Garland, the show's regular team host, reminisced, "People who try to preserve their public image, to act the as they think the public expects them to act rather than as themselves, aren't for this show. Hedy Lamarr did the show and she was just a wreck! I never saw anyone so panicked in my life."[138] Luckily, Barbara's vivacious nature made the hilarious show fun to watch, despite Hedy's distressed behaviour.

At the end of 1962, Barbara appeared in an episode of Alcoa Premiere, "Five, Six, Pick Up Sticks," a 60-minute filmed drama that starred Fred

---

[136] Source: email contact with author.

[137] Source: email contact with author.

[138] Vecchio, Deborah Del. *Beverly Garland – Her Life and Career.* Jefferson: McFarland & Company, Inc., 2013.

Astaire. Also in the cast were her friend, Mickey Rooney, and John Forsythe. The show was aired in January 1963.

She appeared in six other shows on television in 1963. The most memorable are her two guest appearances on *The Beverly Hillbillies*. She played Chickadee Laverne, Jethro's love interest. A newspaper review read, "Jethro gets first-hand advice on courting from Jed and practically kidnaps a buxom burlesque queen and takes her to the Clampett mansion for family approval. The contrast of characters makes for some very funny moments and the blonde babe capitalizes on the contrast for unusual profit to her act. Barbara Nichols is quite funny as the whiningly shrill object of Jethro's affections."

Barbara twisting with Dean Reynolds at Ciro's, 1963.

Let it Ride! Soundtrack recording.

Barbara, Dick Powell, Angie Dickinson and Mamie Van Doren in *The Dick Powell Theatre*, 1962.

Barbara and Buddy Ebsen in *The Beverly Hillbillies*, 1963.

Comedy and Science Fiction

THE MID-1960S WERE VERY PRODUCTIVE years for Barbara. In August 1963, she was signed by producer Jerome Hellman to appear with Peter Sellers in *The World of Henry Orient* (1964). The role was her first casting on the east coast since *Let It Ride!* She arrived in New York on August 25.

Budgeted at $2 million, *The World of Henry Orient* was, according to *The New York Times*, the most expensive movie ever filmed there.

On September 30, Barbara attended a star-studded celebration at the Gaslight Café in Manhattan that marked comedian Jimmy Durante's 50th anniversary in show business. Two days later, she started working on *The World of Henry Orient*. Filming took place in a converted hangar at Long Island's Roosevelt Field airport in Garden City. Barbara was contracted to film one scene with Sellers. Much to her dislike, the director ordered her shower scene to be reshot with a body double, much younger starlet Eva Sloan. In the end, Barbara's scene was cut from the final print entirely.

While in New York, she made guest appearances on *The Tonight Show* with Johnny Carson, and *Girls Talk* hosted by Virginia Graham.

Barbara was once again interviewed about being unmarried. A newspaper article from that period read, "Barbara Nichols' Formula for a Romantic Marriage: 'He'll Live in His House; I'll Live in Mine!'" Barbara stated, "When a married couple starts living under the same roof, what happens is ugh! They start finding out about one another's irritating habits. Then, before you know it, angry words, disillusionment, and divorce . . . I think I can sell the right fellow my His and Hers plan. Maybe he'll read this article and call me up. My telephone number is in the book. I like older men. They've had time to swing, to find out what it's all about. And I admire intelligence, too. Where can I find an intellectual swinger?"[139]

On October 7, 1963, Barbara flew from JFK airport to Los Angeles in order to start working on *The Out-of-Towners* at Warner Bros. She was to play a hotel employee working at the information desk, and had several scenes with Glenn Ford. She was handed some witty lines, and she had a wonderfully funny scene with Glenn. After he picks up her at a newsstand, he nervously tries to check the two of them into a hotel as husband and wife. She silently plays along, and Glenn thinks he has everyone fooled, until the bellboy greets her by her real name and Barbara cheerfully answers.

In December 1964, almost a year after completion, the movie was released as *Dear Heart*, and received poor reviews.

Director Delbert Mann explained why Barbara's wardrobe in the film was kept plain. "This time, I didn't want Barbara to pop out of her dresses. I wanted her to act out of them."

---

[139] *Sunday Herald*, November 10, 1963.

Peter Ford (1945), Glenn's son got to know Barbara on the set. He played the small part of the bellboy. "I got to know Barbara when we made the film together, and afterwards, she used to come to the house. She was a friend of dad's, and they never really dated, but she was just a wonderful gal. She just was a real good spirit and a real fun person."[140]

In winter 1963, Barbara was cast for an episode of *Kraft Suspense Theatre*, which was to be filmed at Universal Studios. She was called upon to play a bimbo that sets up the leading man. Diane McBain, another blonde Warner Bros. contract player, also appeared in the show. She recalled in her autobiography how Barbara, Scott Marlowe, Philip Carey, and she "commiserated about the demise of the contract system ... we shared our troubles about how to reinvent ourselves and take control of our own professional destinies. Barbara's once promising film career hit the skids and she scrambled for television work to survive. Scott's personal life dogged him. He was gay, and the revelation of his affair with Tab Hunter a few years earlier was too much for him to overcome professionally. Philip and I were licking our wounds after being shown the door by Jack Warner."[141]

At the time, Barbara seemed to hold the best cards of that foursome. She was signed to do a cameo part in a new movie and had just wrapped up a movie at MGM. What she didn't know was that these would be the last meaningful assignments in her career.

In late 1963, she worked on a movie at MGM called *Looking for Love*. The movie reunited her with Connie Francis, Jim Hutton, and other cast members of *Where the Boys Are* (1960). Barbara played the arrogant prima donna, Gaye Swinger. One might suggest that the person who came up with that name and persona hinted at Barbara's personal life. Singer Gaye Swinger agrees to endorse Connie's invention, "the lady valet," and a party is given in her honor to publicize it. Not impressed with Connie or the product, Gaye asks Jim, "Now, who do you have to know to get a belt around here?" When

---

[140] Source: telephone conversation with author, 1-19-2015.

[141] McBain, Diane and Michaud, Michael Gregg. *Famous Enough – A Hollywood Memoir*. The BearManor Media: Duncan, Oklahoma, 2014.

she realizes it's Connie who took her place on the *Danny Thomas Show* after she sprained her ankle due to Jim's clumsiness, she angrily leaves the party, threatening Jim. "Accidentally junior, I'm suing you!"

Although Barbara and Connie had a hot affair in 1960, "Fires dimmed out a lot by 1963," John Cohan explained. "Connie got bored very easily in ties like that."[142]

Christopher Riordan met Barbara on the set of *Looking for Love* and recalled a tense moment between Connie and Barbara.

"In the very beginning of 1964, I was asked by a choreographer, Robert Sidney, to report to MGM for a film he was doing with Connie Francis. I had never worked with Mr. Sidney before, but he told me then that he wanted to work with me. I gave it no other thought, as, one, I really didn't want to work as a dancer, and two, if I did dance, I couldn't imagine any other choreographer being as wonderful as Hermes Pan. And I'm very sensitive about my work situation. But Sidney had this very involved number in mind, which included a lot of dangerous things. He needed youth, and he needed strength. What I lacked in years of dance training, I made up for in those two other areas. And so, without auditioning, I was hired.

"This number we were doing was intricate, so hazardous, and had to be timed so perfectly that nearly everyone working on the MGM lot came to the sound stage to watch us rehearse. Well, others in the cast of *Looking for Love* were also curious. So, from time to time we had Susan Oliver, Jim Huton, Joby Baker, and Barbara Nichols sitting in the audience.

"For the most part, Jim and Joby took an occasional glance, but seemed unimpressed. Susan was a bit more interested, but Barbara sat in the audience and made funny little remarks. Since Miss Francis was having trouble enough with the number, she didn't take too kindly to this. Eventually, Sidney had to close the set and ban any more people from coming in."[143]

Another movie that was not very well-received by film critics was director

---

[142] Source: email contact with author.

[143] Used with permission by Mr. Riordan, taken from his Facebook page.

Frank Tashlin's *The Disorderly Orderly* (1964). Comedian Jerry Lewis plays a chaotic orderly, who wreaks havoc in a private rest home/hospital. Barbara plays Miss Marlowe, a bitchy actress, who loves her "vintage" champagne. She must have had a wonderful time playing the sharp-tongued actress who keeps on nagging about everything she's paying for but not getting.

Although the movie bombed, Barbara received a positive review in *The New York Times*. "For our money, the picture has only two hilarious bits, both of them screamingly funny and involving Alice Pearce and Barbara Nichols. The two, playing patients, are listed simply as 'guest stars.' In one scene Mr. Lewis wheels hypochondriac Miss Pearce over the hospital grounds and fights nausea listening to her rhapsodizing about her ills and operations. As for Miss Nichols, the star tries to fix her television set, only to have home-screen 'snow' leak out and whip up a blizzard."[144]

Barbara was thankful to Jerry for not casting her for her curves. She said about it in an interview, "Jerry Lewis is the only one who didn't see me that way. I play a movie star who is in the hospital. It's not a dramatic scene, but at least I'm not doing a striptease for a change."[145]

In 1964, Barbara was in another car accident. She was driving down Mulholland Drive in Hollywood when her car collided with another car. The accident severely damaged her liver. Once again, she needed time to recuperate, but unlike the accident that occurred eight years earlier, there wasn't a warm welcome back into the movie world when she was released. She was out of work for several months, and she was forced to take on a part in a B-movie, *The Human Duplicators* (1965).

Most scenes in Barbara's former movies had been filmed at major studios, but *The Human Duplicators* was low-budget. Although she appeared in a part with more substance than those she had played over the last several years, she still wasn't too happy. The science fiction potboiler was about an alien visiting planet Earth and a scientist who clones people. *The Human Duplicators* was

---

[144] *New York Times*, December 24, 1964.

[145] *Long Island Star-Journal*, July 13, 1964.

co-directed by Hugo Grimaldi, who also produced *Single Room Furnished* (1966) with Jayne Mansfield. Filming took place in and around Los Angeles in autumn 1964. Allied Artists distributed the movie, and it was released on March 3, 1965.

Barbara plays George Nader's girlfriend. About fifteen minutes into the movie, she shares a scene with Hugh Beaumont and George. They discuss the threat of aliens cloning human beings. George takes her to a restaurant. Because he is in real life a closeted gay man, the scene with Barbara is unintentionally funny. The two sit at a table in a cozy restaurant, and George seems distracted.

Barbara comments, "Remember me? I'm the girl you took to dinner."

To which, George replies, "I'm sorry, I guess I was someplace else."

He must have experienced this a lot in his career, especially when the studios made him date their starlet players to keep up a façade of heterosexuality.

Although she must have known *The Human Duplicators* wasn't Oscar material, she still made the most of her role. When she discovers that George is captured and that an android has taken his place, she goes out to investigate. In high heels and with her fur coat on, she follows George's android and almost gets killed when he attacks her. She calls for help, and when the robots have been destroyed and the alien returns to the universe, she runs into the arms of the real George. End of movie.

Producer/director Arthur C. Pierce (1923-1987) also directed other low-budget movies, such as *The Las Vegas Hillbillys* (1966) with Jayne Mansfield and Mamie Van Doren. The latter also starred in his *The Navy vs the Night Monsters* (1966).

Actress Margaret Teele (1941) made her motion picture debut playing one of the nurses. She remembered Grimaldi as a very nice man, who didn't fool around with any of the girls on the movie. In her opinion he was a great director and respectful towards everyone. Miss Teele. "My manager heard about this independent production and he introduced me to the producer of the film, Arthur C. Pierce. Pierce was a very nice man and he immediately developed a major crush on me. He said he wanted me for the leading part in the movie. I took the screen test with Richard Kiel and the director couldn't stop laughing at my performance, but not in a mean way. I'm not easily offended and I understood that I had no acting experience. Because the producer liked me so much, he absolutely wanted me on his picture and wrote another part in it for me. That's how I became one of the nurses."

About the rest of the cast, Margaret remembered, "Dolores Faith, who played the lead of the blind girl, was very aloof, cool and snobby. She stayed separate from anybody else. Richard Kiel and George Nader were the nicest men." About Barbara, Miss Teele remembered a funny anecdote that happened on the set. "Every day, she would come in late, a little bit late, I remember. And she would say, 'Hi everybody!' in that high pitched voice, 'I'm sorry I'm late.' And then she said to George Nader, 'I hope you're not gonna mind, but I ate garlic and onions last night. So I hope you're not gonna mind when we're doing this love scene.' And I remember thinking to myself, 'How could she have done that?'" Margaret continued. "She just seemed like a dingbat, you know what I mean? She seemed kind of goofy to me. I don't remember much about her. She just kind of walked around. She was kind of like an alien. She just seemed like she seemed in the movie. She wasn't unkind or anything. But I don't remember much about her except she was fluffy, I guess that would be the best way to describe her. As a personality, she was just like a fluff ball. She wasn't the kind of person you would sit down with and have a deep conversation with. There's so much time during the making of a movie you know, you sit around a lot. You could talk with Richard Kiel, you could talk with the director and the producer, you could talk with George Nader or other people. But with Barbara, I don't remember that she would necessarily be the type that you would engage in, in any kind of a meaningful conversation."[146]

In December 1964, Earl Wilson recalled, "Barbara Nichols has a handsome twenty-six-year-old Texas boyfriend, Ronnie Graham, American

---

[146] Source: telephone conversation with author, 7-13-2014.

Football player from Rice University. But she got his name changed to Larry Graham because there's a well-known Ronny Graham on Broadway."

This last Graham was the playwright who re-wrote several scenes for *Let It Ride!* in 1961. Barbara's affair with her toy-boy was short-lived.

Barbara started to loathe the fact that she was always typecast. She was cast to play a stripper once more, in a comedy about the funeral business called *The Loved One* (1965). Reverend Glenworthy (Jonathan Winters) needs to reclaim the land that he owns, presently a cemetery, so he can build an old folks home. He has devised a plan to shoot all the bodies into space. The first body they want to exhume and shoot off into space is the husband of grieving widow Barbara. So, his assistant, Robert Morse, visits her at the Zomba Café to try and convince her to let him.

The star-studded cast didn't help to make this black satire a box-office hit. The movie bombed. Just like Jayne Mansfield's scenes, Barbara's work was originally edited out of the movie. Director Tony Richardson decided to cut several scenes after reassuring audience reaction at several screenings.

Variety mentioned the cuts. "No slight was intended to Miss Nichols, who did quite a creditable job as the floozy widow of a defunct astronaut, but a bit of trimming was thought necessary and six minutes went, including all of Miss Nichols' scenes."[147]

Later versions have her scene intact.

Christopher Riordan recalled, "The second time I encountered Miss Nichols was when we were both working on *The Loved One*. I only saw her once, as I believe her scenes were ending, as mine were just beginning to be shot. This time, she seemed rather quiet. But then, with 'that' cast, you wouldn't stand much of a chance at passing remarks. Just having Jonathan Winters doing his 'thing' at every free moment would put the brakes on anyone else trying to get a word into the conversation."[148]

The game show, *Make the Scene,* secured her with a regular income for a

---

[147] October 13, 1965.

[148] Used with permission by Mr. Riordan, taken from his Facebook page.

couple of months. She appeared in fifty-two episodes of the show with actor/stand-up comedian Mickey Manners as regular team captains. The show was hosted by Al Lohman Jr. Barbara and her team had to identify movie clips and famous old stills and act them out. The show ran from Monday through Thursday at 10 p.m. from September 13 until December 9, 1965.

In October 1965, an episode of the popular Western series, *Laredo*, in which she had a good role, aired on television. In "A Question of Discipline," Barbara was reunited with Neville Brand, her co-star from *The Untouchables*.

Neville and his friend, Peter Brown, are both vying for Barbara's attention. She plays Princess, a curvaceous blonde saloon girl. Peter is also being chased by Marlyn Mason, the wife of the owner of a general store. When Barbara and co-star Barbara Werle are fired due to fighting, they need to leave town, and Marlyn decides to leave her husband. Neville and Peter include the three women on their trip.

Actress Marlyn Mason (1940) pleasantly remembered Barbara. "My memory of her brings smiles because she had that funny, brassy way about her and a raucous laugh. I recall Neville teasing her a lot. He had a raucous laugh, too. Most of us actors are just big babies, big kids!"[149]

Barbara's dog, Muffin, also makes an appearance.

A beautiful, slim, and happy-looking Barbara attended a party Jayne Mansfield held to celebrate the birth and christening of her new baby Tony Cimber, on October 31, 1965. Among the other guests were Cesar Romero, Kay Gable—Clark Gable's widow—and Barbara. They had renewed their friendship when they met each other again on the set of *The Loved One*.

---

[149] Source: email contact with author.

The World of Henry Orient, 1963.

Barbara and Glenn Ford on the set of *Dear Heart*, 1964.

Barbara and Glenn Ford in *Dear Heart*, 1964.

Comedy and Science Fiction

Barbara in *Dear Heart*, 1964.

Barbara in *Looking for Love*, 1964.

Barbara with Jim Hutton, Jay C. Flippen and Connie Francis in *Looking for Love*, 1964.

Barbara and Jerry Lewis in *The Disorderly Orderly*, 1964.

Barbara in *The Disorderly Orderly*, 1964.

Barbara with Hugh Beaumont and George Nader in *The Human Duplicators*, 1965.

Barbara and Hugh Beaumont in *The Human Duplicators*, 1965.

Barbara in *The Loved One*, 1965.

Comedy and Science Fiction

Barbara and Nita Talbot at a Hollywood party, 1965.

Decline

IN EARLY 1966, BARBARA SIGNED A CONTRACT with producers Sammy Lewis and Danny Dare to appear in a stage version of *Pal Joey* once again. This time, the Kim Novak part of showgirl Linda English was hers. Yvonne De Carlo played Vera Simpson and singer Frankie Avalon held the part of Joey. The show was performed at the Melodyland Theatre, Anaheim, California starting June 14 and running until September 18.

Barbara had a wonderful time with good friend Yvonne De Carlo, on and off stage. Robert Bouvard (1936) was Yvonne's personal make-up artist and hair dresser on this show and many others. Bouvard thought back, "Yvonne and Barbara seemed to enjoy each other's company. I remember us having lots of laughs together. Frankie stayed with his Vegas crowd most of the time and I didn't get to know him outside of the show. Goldie Hawn was in the chorus. This was before she became famous."

Peter Ford, who knew Barbara for several years through his father's parties, was invited to see the play. "I was dating an actress in the show by the name of Denise Roberts who invited me to see her. Denise was the heir to the Warner Lambert Company fortune, but Denise was pursuing work as an actress. Her mother and sister where there and her mother hosted a big party after the show to which the stars of the show came. It was there I was almost strangled by Barbara Nichols! Denise had invited me to come to see her and Barbara said she would be there, and I said 'oh, that's great' and I went down with a friend of mine called Scotty. We went down to see the play and were invited to a party after the show. It was at a hotel which had a pool. There was lots of alcohol. Barbara had a little bit too much to drink, she grabbed me and she gave me a kiss. She used her tongue, well she French-kissed me! Her tongue was like a snake," Peter laughs. "She was very, very passionate and I think she was caught up in the moment, you know with the party and the alcohol. She put her tongue so deep in my throat that I thought she was going to strangle me. She stayed on it a while, it wasn't about just a little thing. And I said, 'Barbara, what are you doing?!'"

Freed from her sturdy grip, Peter and his friend moved towards the pool.

"Afterwards, everyone was pretty much loaded with alcohol and this girl at the party, called Goldie Hawn, said to my friend and me, 'Let's go swimming.' Goldie took off all of her clothes except for her underwear and she and my friend, Scotty, and I jumped into the swimming pool and we were swimming basically nude in the pool, but that's the kind of party it was.

"Barbara used to come to the house afterwards, we had a big mansion in Beverly Hills and dad had a lot of parties there. Elizabeth Taylor used to come, Richard Burton, Gregory Peck, Kirk Douglas. He'd have these huge parties, and Barbara used to come to the parties, she'd be escorted by somebody. I'd see her through the years and she was just a wonderful gal who had a great sense of humor, did not take herself seriously at all. That party was so out of context with her, because she was much older than me. Well she grabbed and she kissed me, but because she was kind of a family friend it was so out of context."[150]

Besides *Pal Joey*, Barbara appeared in a cameo as strip club owner Blossom LaTour in *The Swinger* (1966) with Ann-Margaret. She teaches Ann how to move, while she is performing on stage in her burlesque house, The Pink Pussycat. Ann-Margret is too shy to strip, so to help, Barbara turns on a machine that starts pulling of the feathers of her costume.

She also played a part in two episodes of *Batman* as Maid Marilyn, assistant to the villain, The Archer's, played by Art Carney.

Barbara experienced a devastating loss when her pal, Hollywood reporter Mike Connolly, died at age fifty-two on November 18. He had supported her career in his newspaper columns and had been a drinking buddy and confidant for more than ten years. To cover up his homosexuality, Barbara had been his most frequent date in the late 1950s. He liked Barbara because she was "bawdy and boozy."[151]

Barbara was signed to do summer stock in the summer of 1967. She toured the east coast in *The Wonderful World of Burlesque*. She played a Burlesque professor, who introduces the viewers to several acts, including the routine of specialty dancer Lynn "The Original Garter Girl" O'Neill. Barbara played some comedy skits with comedian and singer Don Potter and straight man Tom Dillon.

In *The Wonderful World of Burlesque*, she also sang "Poor Butterfly," "St. James Infirmary," "You Gotta See Your Momma Every Night" from *The George Raft Story*, "Zip," and "Red Hot Mama" from *Pal Joey*. The show's booklet mentioned, "Needless to say, the show that you will see this evening is not like the show you might see in the back streets of Manhattan. Rather, it is a nostalgic look at the great acts of yesteryear and a tongue-in-cheek glance

---

[150] Telephone conversation with author, 1-19-2015.

[151] Holley, Val. *Mike Connolly and the Manly Art of Hollywood Gossip.* Jefferson: McFarland & Company, Inc., 2003.

at the teasing entre acts which got grandpa into the theatre but which, of course, is not the reason you are here tonight!"

To publicize *The Wonderful World of Burlesque*, Barbara was the guest of Johnny Carson on *The Tonight Show* in July 1967. The way she behaved was a bit too much for Carson. Her incessant chattering, raucous laughter, and interruption of the other guests finally exasperated the easy going Carson, who told her to "Shut up!"

After *The Wonderful World of Burlesque* closed, Lynn O'Neill and her mother, Josephine, stayed in touch with Barbara. They corresponded with each other for the rest of Barbara's life. Barbara called Lynn her "adopted sister."

Just like Barbara, free-spirited Lynn (1918-2010) was from New York. She was a trained ballerina, but made fame in the early 1940s as a Burlesque dancer/striptease dancer. Lynn's manager was her mother Josephine. She travelled with her daughter wherever she performed. Lynn kept performing when she was well into her fifties.

Barbara also talked on the phone with her friend, Dee Drummond on a regular basis. Dee was a confidant, and Barbara relied on her advice in times of trouble and depression. Talking with her friends about the good old days always cheered her up.

Dee's son, Bruce, remembered Barbara visiting them in Florida. "Barbara was the type of lady that when she saw me would pinch my cheek, 'Brucie's sooooo cute' and then bear hug me with that big chest in my face. My Mom had some other friends similar to that, knowing all the Copa and Vegas girls; but Barbara was the best one. So beautiful, vivacious, wonderful. Oh, I forgot her dog—Barbee—can you believe it, Barbara and Barbee! She always had that dog with her. What also stands out is she sort of lived 'in character' a real actress, dramatic and strong."

For Barbara, television and movie work nearly dried up during the late 1960s. She tried to find work, but she seemed forgotten by producers and casting directors.

DECLINE

A newspaper article about talk show host Joey Bishop mentioned her in association with her appearances on *The Tonight Show* with Johnny Carson. "Carson never uses women. He always uses cartoons of them—a Barbara Nichols, a Zsa Zsa [Gabor], the professional ding-a-lings, never an overtly intelligent woman. Just apparently brainless blabbermouths, sexy squirrels who'll yak about anything, no matter how personal."[152]

Never the type to show she was hurt, nor exposing that she felt sorry for herself, Barbara stepped out and partied. Santiago Rodriguez, a young celebrity photographer, spotted her around town and remembered her as being very friendly and cooperative. "As for Barbara Nichols, when I moved out to Los Angeles, she seemed to be just about everywhere, especially in the 1960s and 1970s. I don't remember anything special about the encounters, but do remember she was always more than willing to pose for me, and there was never any problem in getting her to pose with another celebrity nearby (James Stacy, John Russell, Louisa Moritz). She clearly knew the value of press."[153]

In 1967, Barbara was cast in a movie to be shot in Buenos Aires, Argentina. Roger Smith, her friend and Ann-Margret's husband, secured her a small part in *Sette Uomini e un Cervello* (1968), which starred Ann-Margret and Rossano Brazzi, who also wrote the screenplay and directed the movie. Although Barbara was third billed, she only makes two small appearances in this horrific comedy/action movie. At this stage in her career, she took whatever acting work came her way.

Neither Barbara nor Ann-Margret could have foreseen what a disastrous movie Brazzi had produced. In 1970, the movie was released in the United States. For the American version, called *Criminal Affair*, Barbara's voice was dubbed.

Franco Corridoni, the make-up artists working on the film, remembered Barbara as a beautiful woman and a fantastic actress. He also remembered

---

[152] *Chicago Tribune*, December 17, 1967.

[153] Source: email contact with author.

that the wife of one of the producers threatened her husband with a gun at a party for the cast and crew in a hotel in Buenos Aires.[154]

Late 1967, Barbara filmed a scene for the science fiction movie, *The Power* with George Hamilton. MGM had announced plans to produce the movie during its 40th anniversary celebration in 1964. Unlike many announced projects, this one actually got made, and the movie was released on February 21, 1968.

Suzanne Pleshette was cast as the female lead. She stayed clear of Barbara; the two did not meet on set. Barbara's long-time friend, Yvonne De Carlo, and former fling Michael Rennie, were also in the cast.

Barbara plays the roadhouse waitress wife of a gas station attendant (Aldo Ray). She shares a four-minute scene with George and Aldo. She flirts with George and tells him she regrets that she left New York for this gas station-tavern in the desert town, Joshua Flatt. Her voice in the scene is pleasant and soft instead of her "normal" scratchy speaking voice. Her cousin, Janice Pease, illustrated how different Barbara was from her screen persona. "She was not the character she played; blonde bombshell, etc. She was smart, funny, loving, determined, and talented. Her voice was not what you heard on the screen. I remember when I arrived [to stay at her place] and started talking to Barb, she said, 'Oh my God, no ... you have the Long Island accent!' I worked hard to get rid of it. I didn't know I had an accent and started to work on overcoming my disability."[155]

In 1969, Barbara's only foray in showbiz had been an appearance in an episode of *Hawaii Five-O*. She's seen wearing heavy make-up in her role as a double-crossing club owner called Betsy. Her voice sounds husky but more natural than in her many other appearances. Betsy was a good part, but no other work offers came her way that year.

Barbara Luna (1939) also appeared on that episode of *Hawaii Five-O* and remembered working with Barbara Nichols vividly. "One does NOT forget

---

[154] Source: email contact with author.

[155] Source: email contact with author.

working with Barbara Nichols! And I mean that in a fond memory category." Barbara Luna continued. "Barbara Nichols was an interesting character, but quite an adorable one. Her choice of words certainly could make a truck driver blush, which she was able to accomplish every morning in the make-up room while we were filming *Hawaii Five-O*. When she walked in, it wasn't just a simple good morning, it was 'How the fuck is everyone today, holy shit, I couldn't sleep a fucking wink last night and where's the gawd damn coffee!' The sweet gay make-up man would blush and giggle and try to calm himself while the rest of us just broke out in laughter. I'm laughing just thinking about the scenario. She loved to curse however, Barbara wasn't vulgar, it was just who she was, a darling caricature of herself. If I had to portray a blonde hooker with a heart, Barbara Nichols would have been my perfect image!"[156]

In the absence of further work, Barbara's partying and use of alcohol intensified. Pamela Wells remembered seeing her with a couple of presumably gay girlfriends at a male gay bar in West Hollywood. "I met her around 1970 or so, when I was in the Theatre Department at UCLA and going to gay bars in West Hollywood at night. I didn't wear a bra then and had on a sort of see-through blouse. She and her girlfriends, all talking in a circle, looked at me a lot!"[157]

Christopher Riordan remembered, "It was quite a while until I saw Barbara again. In the meantime, I had heard that she went through a rather rough love affair. I know her career wasn't going as she wished. She was getting older and that, combined with not taking great care of herself, was taking a toll. I'd see her at my friend Nicky Nichols (no relation) restaurant, The Garden District. She'd come in like the old Barbara: sweet, quiet, and well-mannered. Later in the evening, she got louder, a bit more dishevelled, sometimes even going over to the other booths and tables and talking to the customers. One night, they couldn't drag her out of the bar to return to her booth for her meal. She was heavily into conversation with a couple of men at

---

[156] Source: email contact with author.
[157] www.imdb.com

the bar—and heavily into her cocktails. I remember feeling very sad for her. Little did we know that aside from the mental pain she was going through, she had a lot of physical pain, as well."[158]

Rob Matteson, who worked at The Garden District at the time, knew Barbara and met her when she visited the restaurant. He remembered that she usually came at lunch with Don Cook and Alan Taylor.

Taylor Pero, once Lana Turner's personal manager and confidante, remembered, "Just the mention of The Garden District brings back so many memories. It was my second home for years. I often saw Barbara Nichols walking up La Cienega Boulevard and she always looked like she was wearing too much makeup and was way overdressed for daytime... as if expecting the cameras to roll at any second. Not an unusual sight in Hollywood."[159]

Times changed quickly. All of a sudden, Barbara found herself unwanted and old. She was regarded as a relic of the old Hollywood. New names were preoccupying showbiz gossip and new faces were taking over the parts that Barbara had played years before.

Lauren Angelich, a teenager at the time, lived next door to Barbara in West Hollywood, at the time. She witnessed Barbara's decline from depression and alcoholism. Lauren found her vulgar and ill mannered. "She had a poodle she would not walk on a leash. I had a large Irish setter, and her dog would bark and throw a fit when he saw my dog. She acted like I didn't have the right to walk my dog and, at one point, her dog ran and attacked my dog. He was actually hanging from his neck and I practically kicked her dog away and that started a street fight between us. Barbara and I would have screaming matches in the street. I never saw her dressed; she was always in a bathrobe and did not look happy, very 'floozy'-like. She became very promiscuous when drunk, asking men for sex in public."[160]

---

[158] Source: email contact with author.

[159] Source: email contact with author.

[160] Source: email contact with author.

Barbara, Yvonne DeCarlo and Frankie Avalon, 1966.

Barbara in TV's *Batman*, 1966.

Barbara and Barbee Girl, Christmas Card, 1966. (Courtesy of Bruce Blau).

That Kind of Woman

Barbara, Lynne O'Neill - holding Barbara's dog Muffin - and two dancers from *The Wonderful World of Burlesque*, 1967.

Handwritten note to Lynne O'Neill.

Barbara in 1968.

Barbara in TV's *Hawaii Five-O*, 1969.

Barbara and Muffin, 1969.

Barbara in TV's *The Rookies*, 1974.

Health Problems

IN HER EARLY FORTIES, Barbara hoped she'd fall into character roles and that she might be able to excel once more and gain notice again, but that did not happen. Not working on a regular basis made her very unhappy. Her drinking was becoming a big problem. She must have felt her career was never really fulfilled, and maybe she was aware that, by not taking good care of herself, she was not going to be around much longer.

Actor Christopher Riordan remembered meeting Barbara in the early 1970s. "I used to run into her socially. By now, she had gone through several bad romances, and was beginning to lose the figure she once had, and was so proud of. I wanted to like her; and I wouldn't say that I didn't like her, but I didn't like what she would become after several drinks. It seemed as though, after having a few, she told herself that the public wanted her to behave like a loud and obnoxious bimbo. And so, often, she gave it to them. But prior to all those drinks and 'empty conversation,' as she called it, I saw a sad and lonely girl that just didn't seem to be able to find her way to being the person she either thought she wanted to be, or the person she figured she 'could' be."[161]

Michael B. Druxman was Barbara's publicist for a couple of months in 1971 and 1972. "Back then, I would go after 'names' who were no longer hot. I'd get their home numbers and call them. Sometimes I'd get lucky and pick up a client."

That's how Barbara came in contact with Druxman, but their collaboration was short-lived. Druxman said, "We did not get along. She liked her booze too much. She would have too much to drink, call me up and yell . . . about nothing. She was one of the few clients that I fired. About a month after we parted company, I saw her standing in line for the first screening of *The Godfather* (1972) on opening day [in March], but we didn't speak. That was the last time I saw her. Actually, she was a very good actress, but I think she was frustrated at being typed in one kind of role."[162]

In summer 1972, Barbara worked on a film for Walt Disney. *Charley and the Angel* (1973) is situated in the 1930s and features Fred MacMurray as a workaholic husband and father. MacMurray encounters an angel, who tells him he has to spend more time with his family rather than being busy making money all the time. Barbara plays the owner of a bar where alcoholic beverages are sold illegally.

Kathleen Cody (1954) also appeared in the film. She remembered being thrilled when she heard Barbara had joined the cast. "My introduction to Barbara by the director of our film was very brief but quite memorable to me. I was as excited as Vince McEveety [the director] that we had 'the' Barbara Nichols joining the cast of *Charley and the Angel*! It was wonderful getting to meet her however briefly that day on set and she was just as I expected.

---

[161] Source: email contact with author.

[162] Source: email contact with author.

Health Problems

Dressed in her wardrobe for the scene where she plays the role of a madam at a Speakeasy club, she was all smiles, brash talk, and loud laughter. And of course, as 'Monroesque' as ever."[163]

Charley and the Angel went into general release on March 23, 1973. Although it was another relatively small role, Barbara made the most of it, and critics took notice. *The New York Times* mentioned her in its review. "Little sparkle or wit is accorded as appealing a family as any papa could wish. But Cloris Leachman as his wife, Kathleen Cody, Vincent Van Patten and little Scott Kolden do pleasantly by humdrum material. The same goes for Harry Morgan as the wry visitor from above and, very minutely, Barbara Nichols."

By the mid-1970s, Barbara had developed a life-threatening liver disease, because of the Long Island car accident in 1957 that had led to the loss of her spleen, and the other serious car accident in Southern California in 1964 that had led to a torn liver. Complications set in, and she was forced to slow down her career.

Besides her health problems, along with other actors of her generation, the 1970s were bumpy years. She hit hard times, and things were rough all over. Her 1973 diary shows that she regularly visited the hospital and even had to skip appointments with friends. Because of her poor health, she often felt too tired and depressed, and she preferred staying home and drinking to going out. She begged cousin Janice to come and live with her.

Janice told later, "In the mid-1970s, she drank because work was scant for her as she was type cast. She was lonely, for sure. She begged me to move to California to live with her. But I was only nineteen or twenty and didn't consider it. I truly wish I was older when she asked."[164]

In 1974, Barbara moved from 8558 Hollywood Drive to her new home on 8033 Hollywood Blvd. in Los Angeles. She was cast in two television shows and landed a starring role in a B-movie, *The Photographer*.

In *The Photographer* (1974), Barbara plays a promiscuous mother to a

---

[163] Source: email contact with author.
[164] Source: email contact with author.

photographer (Michael Callan). He blames her for his gravelly voice from a childhood incident when one of her many lovers caught him spying and choked him until his throat was damaged beyond repair. He now has a deep hatred for women and, therefore, kills his models and photographs them as they die.

Director William Byron Hillman remembered Barbara pleasantly. "Babs was great to work with. Great sense of humor, and regardless, she knew her lines and came to the set with giggles and jokes. She told stories about everyone she ever worked with."

Hillman also experienced what her alcoholism did to her. "Sadly, I was one of the last to work with Barbara on a film. She was starting to slide into bad habits and the drinking disease started to take a toll. She never missed a line, even when the drink had all but consumed her. She snuck drinks onto the set after promising not to. It came in water bottles, can drinks and anything she could use to hide it from me."

Nevertheless, Hillman has pleasant memories of her. "Bottom line, I loved working with her. She always had a smile, a joke to tell, a story to whisper, endless tales, sassy dialog, and such fun to work with."

Barbara respected Hillman, and he respected her. Out of that respect, he confronted her with her drinking habits and demanded that it not influence her work. "She promised she would never miss a line or be late, and she wasn't. We shot one scene with Michael Callan and Babs fighting. She was playing his mother. We rehearsed, and then she went to her dressing room. While I got the next set lit, she got into wardrobe and was waiting for me on the main set. She was sitting straight up and was ready. We shot the scene and only did two takes. It was a great exchange of dialog. Both characters were angry and shouting. When we finished, I thanked her and wondered why she didn't stand up. It was only then the wardrobe and makeup people told me she had begged them to strap her to the chair so she wouldn't fall over. She couldn't walk, but by God she knew her lines and delivered a great take. One of the best scenes in the film. They unstrapped her and she had to be carried to her dressing room."

Health Problems

Hillman concluded, "I never told anyone that story before, but I know Barbara wouldn't mind me doing so. She would laugh, say, 'That's true, but I didn't miss a line!' And then, she would laugh again. She was the ultimate pro. Came from the old school and did her job. I think everyone who worked with her enjoyed the moment."[165]

In a letter dated December 30, 1974, Barbara writes in sloppy handwriting to Lynn O'Neill and her mother, Josephine, that she isn't able to visit them because of the premiere of her new movie. She also mentions one of the TV shows she was in.

"Sorry I haven't written, but I don't even write to mom and dad whom I love very much. I called them when my *Rookies* show was on. Hope you saw it. I played a stripper who wouldn't strip on Christmas, because it was a holy day. Mother and dad called me, too—and of course, we always talk too long—show business is lousy everywhere, as you know they just don't write parts for us... The only way I would come back to New York is to do stock or one of those Dinner theatre shows. I just don't have an agent for that. I need a secretary like you—would be wonderful to do something with you. Maybe you know somebody fun with the Shiffrin Agency in LA."[166]

Her next movie assignment was for a star-studded comedy about a German shepherd dog that becomes a famous movie star and touches the lives of the people he meets. In *Won Ton: The Dog Who Saved Hollywood* (1976), she plays Victor Mature's girlfriend.

On September 18, Barbara shot her scene with Victor. About him, she said, "I always had a crush on him from all those Betty Grable movies. And he still looks great. I said to him, 'I wish I had known you in your prime.' And Vic said, 'I can still turn you on.' My answer, 'You do.'"[167] Other cameo parts were taken by Barbara's former co-stars Tab Hunter and Peter Lawford, and friends Yvonne De Carlo and Jack Carter.

---

[165] Source: email contact with author.
[166] Extract from a letter by Barbara.
[167] *L.A. Herald Examiner*, November 16, 1975.

The film was shot in summer 1975. The photos that were taken of Barbara during this production show an aging woman with signs of illness in her face. By then, her health was deteriorating rapidly. Most likely, her severe drinking combined with diminished health after the car accidents were what caused her health to decay this fast. It seemed inevitable that something had to give.

After principal photography was concluded, Paramount held a wrap party for the cast and crew. The day after the party, Barbara called the *Los Angeles Herald-Examiner* to give them a funny story about comedian George Jessel, who had been trying to date her for some time. "I always tell him I'm too old for him, but last night at the party I gave him my telephone number. So, early this morning, the phone rings, and its George, who says, 'Is this Kelly, the beautiful blonde I met last night?'" Barbara assured him in no uncertain terms that he had gotten his girlfriends mixed up. She finally relented and accepted to have dinner with Jessel.

In April 1976, *Hollywood Reporter* said that an entire episode of *The Merv Griffin Show* was devoted to promoting the film. Among the cast members appearing on the show were Barbara, Rory Calhoun, Bruce Dern, Andy Divine, and Fritz Feld.

On May 26, 1976, Barbara attended the premiere at Grauman's Chinese Theatre in Hollywood. Together with her hairdresser and friend, Bill Zappia, she enjoyed the evening. The photos of the event showed her smiling and happy with the attention given to her.

About his participation in the movie, Tab Hunter mentioned, "You do those things, you just survive. It was far from a great movie." He didn't meet Barbara on this film, but remembered her with great fondness, having worked with her several years earlier. "I remember that she had this wonderful laugh, it was just light and sparkling. And she was always a very upbeat person, but you felt there was a sadness about her the same time. The last time I saw Barbara [in the mid-1960s], I was in a department store going to pick something up, and I ran into Barbara. She was wandering through the store, buying something. It was just so nice to see her and to reconnect with her, because she just was a real touching person. She's one of those people you wanted to know, you wanted to know more about her. She was a very private kind of person, but she was also very outgoing to people she met, which I loved. Because a lot of people build that wall, a barrier around themselves. But that was not Barbara at all."[168]

In summer 1976, Barbara was rushed to Cedar Sinai Hospital in Los Angeles, where she fell into a coma. She awoke for a few days just before Labor Day, but sank back shortly after.

Her friend, Johnny Clark, said she had been cheered by hundreds of letters from fans but heard from only one colleague in the industry—Frank Sinatra.

Julia Nickerauer recalled, "They didn't expect her to last the night, but she came out of it the day before Labor Day and I spoke with her. She said she was sick. The next day, she relapsed into semi-coma and never woke up."

Barbara died of liver failure on October 6 at the age of forty-seven. Funeral arrangements were being handled by Jacobsen's Funeral Parlor of Huntington Station, where a service was held on Monday, October 11. The next day, she was interred at Pinelawn Memorial Park in Farmingdale, New York.

George and Julia chose the following prayer to be printed on the gift Mass cards from Barbara's wake: "The Lord is my Sheppard: I shall not want. He maketh me to lie down in green pastures: He restoreth my soul: He leadeth me in the path of righteousness for his names sake. Yea, though I walk through the valley of the shadow of death, I will fear no evil; for thou art with me. Thou preparest a table before me in the presence of my enemies: thou anointest my head with oil: my cup runneth over. Surely goodness and mercy shall follow me all the days of my life: and I will dwell in the house of the Lord forever." (Twenty-third Psalm).

Alcohol and depression were bad combinations, and dwelling in the past made Barbara completely miserable. She felt she never 'made it.' She'd

---

[168] Source: telephone conversation with author, 11-17-2015.

confided to her friends that she wanted a career like Marilyn Monroe had. Friends, who spoke with her in the days before her death, said they were amazed she didn't commit suicide, because she was that miserable. It was especially sad for her close friends to witness Barbara's decline. Many still remembered her as the sweet, fun and caring person she had always been to them.

John Cohan reminisced, "She didn't have a happy ending and was very depressed. No one was there when she needed support from people she considered friends and co-workers from the old days."[169]

After Barbara died, her cousin, Egbert Carpenter, traveled to her parent's house. While there, he took a phone call. It was actor Glenn Ford, who called Barbara's parents to express his sympathy.

At the time, Barbara's long-time friend Paula Stewart wasn't speaking with her anymore, but she regretted that it had to come this far. "Barbara knew her own character's value and she played the role extremely well, in my estimation. In her last years, she got more self-destructive with the alcohol. It became uncomfortable to be around her staggering and incoherence. Much as I wanted to help, she was out of control and it became necessary to avoid her. That was her Achilles heel and it killed her. What a loss, so talented, and kind hearted."[170]

According to her family, she loved everything about show business and had lived solely for her career. "She just loved it all," her mother recalled. "She was happiest when she was working."[171]

When Barbara's mother was interviewed after her daughter's passing, she remarked on the marriage subject: "She always figured the career would be a problem, unless the person was in the same business, but I think she was sorry she didn't marry."[172]

---

[169] Source: email contact with author.
[170] Source: email contact with author.
[171] *Long Island Press*, October 7, 1976.
[172] *Long Island Press*, October 7, 1976.

Health Problems

Her parents died within several months of each other, years after Barbara's own passing. Her mother Julia died, ninety-one years old, on June 26, 1997. George Nickerauer died on October 30, 1997, age eighty-nine.

Barbara at home, 1971.

Mamie Van Doren, Peter Marshall and Barbara, late 1971.

Barbara backstage with Martin Milner and Gary Crosby, *Adam-12*, 1972.

Barbara in *Charley and the Angel*, 1973.

Barbara in 1972. (Courtesy of Bruce Blau).

Barbara with Eddie Andrews and Harold Stone in *The Photographer*, 1974.

Barbara in a publicity photo for *Won Ton Ton, the Dog Who Saved Hollywood*, 1976.

Barbara at the *Won Ton Ton* Party, with Bill Zappia.

Barbara's mother, Julia Nickerauer behind her foster kids with on the left (partly) Richard Voorhees, 1977. (Courtesy of Janice Pease).

Filmography

River of No Return
1954 – 20th Century Fox
91 minutes - color
Producer: Stanley Rubin. Director: Otto Preminger. Screenplay: Frank Fenton, based on a story by Louis Lantz. Music: Cyril J. Mockridge. Editor: Louis R. Loefler. Make-up: Ben Nye. Photography: Joseph La Shelle. Sound: Bernard Freericks, Roger Heman.
Cast: Robert Mitchum *(Matt Calder)*; Marilyn Monroe *(Kay Weston)*; Rory Calhoun *(Harry Weston)*; Tommy Rettig *(Mark Calder)*; Murvyn Vye *(Dave Colby)*; Douglas Spencer *(Sam Benson)*; Larry Chance (Young

Punk); John Doucette *(Man in Saloon)*; Will Wright *(Trader)*; Don Beddoe *(Ben)*; Geneva Gray *(Dance Hall Girl)*; Jarma Lewis *(Dance Hall Girl)*; Ann McCrea *(Dance Hall Girl)*; **Barbara Nichols** *(Dance Hall Girl)*.

Manfish
1956 – United Artists

76 minutes – color

Producer: W. Lee Wilder. Director: W. Lee Wilder. Screenplay: Joel Murcott, based on the stories *The Gold Bug* and *The Tell-Tale Heart* by Edgar Allan Poe. Music: Albert Elms. Editor: Gerald Turney-Smith. Photography: Scotty Welbourne. Sound: Frank Gallagher.

Cast: John Bromfield *(Captain Brannigan)*; Lon Chaney Jr. *(Swede)*; Victor Jory *(Profesor Walter Fenton)*; **Barbara Nichols** *(Mimi)*; Tessa Prendergast *(Alita)*; Eric Coverly *(Chavez)*; Vincent Chang *(Domingo)*; Theodore Purcell *(Big Boy)*; Vere Johns *(Bianco)*; Jack Lewis *(Warren)*; Arnold Shanks *(Aleppo)*; Clyde Hoyte *(Calypso)*.

Miracle in the Rain
1956 - Warner Bros.

108 minutes – black and white

Producer: Frank P. Rosenberg. Director: Rudolph Maté. Screenplay: Ben Hecht. Music: Frank Waxman. Editor: Thomas Reilly. Make-up: Gordon Bau. Photography: Russell Metty. Sound: Robert B. Lee.

Cast: Jane Wyman *(Ruth Wood)*; Van Johnson *(Pvt. Arthur Hugenon)*; Peggie Castle *(Millie Kranz)*; Fred Clark *(Steven Jalonik)*; Eileen Heckart *(Grace Ullman)*; Josephine Hutchinson *(Agnes Wood)*; **Barbara Nichols** *(Arlene Parker Witchy)*; Alan King *(Sgt. Gilbert Parker)*; William Gargan *(Harry Wood)*; Marcel Dalio *(Marcel, a Waiter)*; George Givot *(Headwaiter)*; Paul Picerni *(Priest)*; Halliwell Hobbes *(Ely B. Windgate)*; Roxanne Arlen *(Cathy Wicklow)*.

The Wild Party

1956 – United Artists

91 minutes – black and white

Producer: Sidney Harmon, Philip Yordan. Director: Harry Horner. Screenplay: John McPartland. Music: Buddy Bregman. Editor: Richard C. Meyer. Make-up: Gustaf Norin. Photography: Sam Leavitt. Sound: Harold Lewis.

Cast: Anthony Quinn *(Tom Kupfen);* Carol Ohmart *(Erica London);* Arthur Franz *(Lt. Arthur Mitchell);* Jay Robinson *(Gage Freeposter);* Kathryn Grant *(Honey);* Nehemiah Persoff *(Kicks Johnson);* Paul Stewart *(Ben Davis);* Nestor Paiva *(Branson);* Maureen Stephenson *(Ellen);* Michael Ross *(Bouncer);* James Bronte *(Bartender);* William Phipps *(Wino);* Joseph J. Greene *(Fat Man);* **Barbara Nichols** *(Sandy);* Jana Mason *(Singer).*

Beyond a Reasonable Doubt

1956 – RKO

80 minutes – black and white

Producer: Bert E. Friedob. Director: Fritz Lang. Screenplay: Douglas Morrow. Music: Herschel Burke Gilbert. Editor: Gene Fowler Jr. Make-up: Lou LaCava. Photography: William Snyder. Sound: Terry Kellum, Jimmy Thompson.

Cast: Dana Andrews *(Tom Garrett);* Joan Fontaine *(Susan Spencer);* Sidney Blackmer *(Austin Spencer);* Arthur Franz *(Bob Hale);* Philip Bourneuf *(District Attorney oy Thompson);* Edward Binns *(Lt. Kennedy);* Shepperd Strudwick *(Jonathan Wilson);* Robin Raymond *(Terry Larue);* **Barbara Nichols** *(Dolly Moore);* William Lester *(Charlie Miller);* Dan Seymour *(Greco);* Rusty Lane *(Judge);* Joyce Taylor *(Joan Williams);* Trudy Wroe *(Hatcheck* Girl).

The King and Four Queens

1956 – United Artists

86 minutes – color

Producer: David Hempstead. Director: Raoul Walsh. Screenplay: Richard Alan Simmons and Margaret Fitts, based on the novel by Margaret Fitts. Music: Alex North. Editor: Louis R. Loeffler. Make-up: Frank Prehoda, Don Roberson. Photography: Lucien Ballard. Sound: Jack Solomon.

Cast: Clark Gable *(Dan Kehoe)*; Eleanor Parker *(Sabina McDade)*; Jo Van Fleet *(Ma McDade)*; Jean Willes *(Ruby McDade)*; **Barbara Nichols** *(Birdie McDade)*; Sara Shane *(Oralie McDade)*; Roy Roberts *(Sheriff Tom Larrabee)*; Arthur Shields *(Padre)*; Jay C. Flippen *(Bartender)*; Florenz Ames *(Josiah Sweet, Undertaker)*; Chuck Roberson *(Posseman)*.

Sweet Smell of Success
1957 – United Artists
96 minutes – black and white
Producer: James Hill. Director: Alexander Mackendrick. Screenplay: Clifford Odets, Ernest Lehman, based on the novella by Ernest Lehman. Music: Elmer Bernstein. Editor: Alan Crosland Jr. Make-up: Robert Schiffer. Photography: James Wong Howe. Sound: Robert Carlisle.

Cast: Burt Lancaster *(J.J. Hunsecker)*; Tony Curtis *(Sidney Falco)*; Susan Harrison *(Susan Hunsecker)*; Martin Milner *(Steve Dallas)*; Jeff Donnell *(Sally)*; Sam Levene *(Frank D'Angelo)*; Joe Frisco *(Herbie Temple)*; **Barbara Nichols** *(Rita)*; Emile Meyer *(Lieutenant Harry Kello)*; Edith Atwater *(Mary)*; Jay Adler *(Manny Davis)*; Lewis Charles *(Al Evans)*; Lawrence Dobkin *(Leo Bartha)*; Joseph Leon *(Joe Robard)*; Autumn Russell *(Linda James)*.

The Pajama Game
1957 – Warner Bros.
101 minutes – color
Producer: George Abbott, Stanley Donen. Director: George Abbott, Stanley Donen. Screenplay: George Abbott, Richard Bissell, based on the novel by Richard Bissell. Music: Ray Heindorf, Howard Jackson. Editor:

William Ziegler. Make-up: Gordon Bau. Photography: Harry Stradling. Sound: M.A. Merrick, Dolph Thomas.

Cast: Doris Day *(Babe Williams)*; John Raitt *(Sid Sorokin)*; Carol Haney *(Gladys Hotchkiss)*; Eddie Foy Jr. *(Vernon Hines)*; Reta Shaw *(Mabel)*; **Barbara Nichols** *(Poopsie)*; Thelma pelish *(Mae)*; Jack Straw *(Prez)*; Ralph Dunn *(Myron Hasler)*; Owen Martin *(Max)*; Buzz Miller *(Dancer)*; Kenneth LeRoy *(Dancer)*; Harvey Evans *(Dancer)*; Drusilla Davis *(Dancer)*; Larri Thomas *(Dancer)*; Dolores Starr *(Dancer)*; Kathy Marlowe *(Holly)*.

Pal Joey

1957- Columbia

111 minutes – color

Producer: Fred Kohlmar. Director: George Sidney. Screenplay: Dorothy Kingsley, from the musical play book by John O'Hara. Music: Nelson Riddle, George Duning. Editor: Viola Lawrence, Jerome Thoms. Make-up: Ben Lane, Robert J. Schiffer. Photography: Harold Lipstein. Sound: Franklin Hansen.

Cast: Rita Hayworth *(Vera Prentice-Simpson)*; Frank Sinatra *(Joey Evans)*; Kim Novak *(Linda English)*; **Barbara Nichols** *(Gladys)*; Bobby Sherwood *(Ned Galvin)*; Hank Henry *(Mike Miggins)*; Elizabeth Patterson *(Mrs. Casey)*; Frank Sully *(Barker)*; Connie Graham *(Stripper)*; Rita Barrett *(Stripper)*; Barry Bernard *(Butler)*; Barrie Chase *(Dancer)*; Judy Dan *(Hat Check Girl)*; Ellie Kent *(Carol)*; Mara McAfee *(Sabrina)*; Bek Nelson *(Lola)*; Betty Utey *(Patsy)*.

Ten North Frederick

1958 – 20th Century Fox

102 minutes – black and white

Producer: Charles Brackett. Director: Phillip Dunne. Screenplay: Phillip Dunne, based on the novel by John O'Hara. Music: Leigh Harline. Editor: David Bretherton. Make-up: Ben Nye. Photography: Joe MacDonald. Sound: Alfred Bruzlin, Harry M. Leonard.

Cast: Gary Cooper *(Joseph B. Chapin);* Diane Varsi *(Ann Chapin);* Suzy Parker *(Kate Drummond);* Geraldine Fitzgerald *(Edith Chapin);* Tom Tully *(Mike Slattery);* Ray Stricklyn *(Joby Chapin);* Linda Watkins *(Peg Slattery);* Philip Ober *(Lloyd Williams);* John Emery *(Paul Donaldson);* Stuart Withman *(Charely Bongiorno);* **Barbara Nichols** *(Stella);* Helen Wallace *(Marian Jackson);* Jo Morrow *(Waitress);* Nolan Leary *(Harry Jackson).*

The Naked and the Dead
1958 – RKO/Warner Bros.
131 minutes – color
Producer: Paul Gregory. Director: Raoul Walsh. Screenplay: Denis Sanders, Terry Sanders, based on the novel by Norman Mailer. Music: Bernard Herrmann. Editor: Arthur P. Schmidt. Make-up: Allan Snyder. Photography: Joseph LaShelle. Sound: Robert B. Lee.
Cast: Aldo Ray *(Sergeant Sam Croft);* Cliff Robertson *(Lieutenant Robert Hearn);* Raymond Massey *(General Cummings);* Lily St. Cyr *(Wilma Mae aka Lily);* **Barbara Nichols** *(Mildred Croft);* William Campbell *(Brown);* James Best *(Rhidges);* Joey Bishop *(Roth);* Jerry Paris *(Goldstein);* Robert Gist *(Red);* L.Q. Jomes *(Woodrow Wilson);* Casey Adams *(Colonel Dalleson);* John Berardino *(Captain Mantelli);* John Close *(Captain);* Alan Austin *(Lieutenant).*

That Kind of Woman
1959 – Paramount
92 minutes – black and white
Producer: Marcello Girosi, Carlo Ponti. Director: Sidney Lumet. Screenplay: Walter Bernstein, based on a story by Robert Lowry. Music: Daniele Amfitheatrof. Editor: Howard Smith. Make-up: George Fiala, Robert Jiras. Photography: Boris Kaufman. Sound: Howard Beals.
Cast: Sophia Loren *(Kay);* Tab Hunter *(Red);* Jack Warden *(George Kelly);* **Barbara Nichols** *(Jane);* Keenan Wynn *(Harry Corwin);* George Sanders

(A.L.); Bea Arthur *(WAC)*; Mary Grace Canfield *(WAC)*; Jeremy Slate *(Sailor)*; Stephen Bolster *(Sailor)*; Raymond Bramley *(General)*; John Fiedler *(Soldier)*; Stefan Gierasch *(Soldier)*; Harold Grau *(Fisherman)*.

Woman Obsessed
1959 – 20th Century Fox
103 minutes – color
Producer: Sydney Boehm. Director: Henry Hathaway. Screenplay: Sydney Boehm, based on the novel by John Mantley. Music: Hugo Friedhofer. Editor: Robert L. Simpson. Make-up: Ben Nye. Photography: William C. Mellor. Sound: W.D. Flick, Harry M. Leonard.
Cast: Susan Hayward *(Mary Sharron)*; Stephen Boyd *(Fred Carter)*; **Barbara Nichols** *(Mayme Radzevitch)*; Dennis Holmes *(Robbie Sharron)*; Theodore Bikel *(Dr. R. W. Gibbs)*; Ken Scott *(Sergeant Le Moyne)*; James Philbrook *(Henri)*; Florence MacMichael *(Mrs. Bedelia Gibbs)*; Mary Carroll *(Mrs. Campbell)*; Arthur Franz *(Tom Sharron)*; Akan Austin *(Fire Warden)*; Richard Monahan *(Store Clerk)*; Jack Raine *(Ian Campbell)*.

The Scarface Mob
1959 – Desilu Productions
102 minutes – black and white
Producer: Quinn Martin. Director: Phil Karlson. Screenplay: Paul Monash. Music: Wilbur Hatch. Editor: Robert L. Swanson. Make-up: Edwin Butterworth. Photography: Charles Straumer. Sound: Keith W. Safford.
Cast: Robert Stack *(Eliot Ness)*; Keenan Wynn *(Joe Fuselli)*; **Barbara Nichols** *(Brandy LaFrance)*; Pat Crowley *(Betty Anderson)*; Bill Williams *(Martin Flaherty)*; Neville Neville *(Al Capone)*; Joe Mantell *(George Ritchie)*; Bruce Gordon *(Frank Nitti)*; Peter Leeds *(LaMarr Kane)*; Eddie Firestone *(Eric Hansen)*; Robert Osterloh *(Tom Kopka)*; Paul Dubov *(Jack Rossman)*; Abel Fernandez *(William Youngfellow)*; Paul Picerni *(Tony Liguri)*.

Who Was That Lady?
1960 – Columbia

115 minutes – black and white

Producer: Norman Krasna. Director: George Sidney. Screenplay: Norman Krasna, based on his play *Who Was That Lady I Saw You With?* Music: André Previn. Editor: Viola Lawrence. Make-up: Ben Lane. Photography: Harry Stradling. Sound: James Flaster.

Cast: Tony Curtis *(David Wilson)*; Dean Martin *(Michael Haney)*; Janet Leigh *(Ann Wilson)*; James Whitmore *(Harry Powell)*; John McIntire *(Bob Doyle)*; **Barbara Nichols** *(Gloria Coogle)*; Joi Lansing (Florence Coogle); Larry Keating *(Parker)*; Larry Storch *(Orenov)*; Simon Oakland *(Belka)*; Barbara Hines *(Foreign Exchange Student)*; Marion Javits *(Miss Mellish)*; Michael Lane *(Glinka)*; Jack Benny *(Mr. Cosgrove)*; Larri Thomas *(Dancing Girl)*.

Where the Boys Are
1960 – MGM

99 minutes – color

Producer: Joe Pasternak. Director: Henry Levin. Screenplay: George Wells, based on the novel by Glendon Swarthout. Music: George Stoll. Editor: Fredric Steinkamp. Make-up: William Tuttle. Photography: Robert Bronner. Sound: Franklin Milton.

Cast: Dolores Hart *(Merritt Andrews)*; George Hamilton *(Ryder Smith)*; Yvette Mimieux *(Melanie Tolman)*; Jim Hutton *(TV Thompson)*; Connie Francis *(Angie)*; Paula Prentiss *(Tuggle Carpenter)*; **Barbara Nichols** *(Lola Fandango)*; Frank Gorshin *(Basil)*; Chill Wills *(Police Captain)*; Rory Harrity *(Franklin)*; Percy Helton *(Fairview Motel Manager)*; John Brennan *(Dill)*.

The George Raft Story
1961 – Allied Artists

106 minutes – black and white

Producer: Ben Schwalb. Director: Joseph M. Newman. Screenplay: Crane Wilbur. Music: Jeff Alexander. Editor: George White. Make-up: Norman Pringle. Photography: Carl Guthrie. Sound: Ralph Butler.

Cast: Ray Danton *(George Raft)*; Jayne Mansfield *(Lisa Lang)*; Julie London *(Sheila Patton)*; Barrie Chase *(June Tyler)*; **Barbara Nichols** *(Texas Guinan)*; Frank Gorshin *(Moxie Cusack)*; Margo Moore *(Ruth Harris)*; Brad Dexter *(Benny 'Bugsy' Siegel)*; Neville Neville *(Al Capone)*; Robert Strauss *(Frenchie)*; Herschel Bernardi *(Sam)*; Joe De Santis *(Frankie Donatella)*; Jack Lambert *(Jerry Fitzpatrick)*; Argentina Brunetti *(Mrs. Raft)*; Robert H. Harris *(Harvey)*.

House of Women
1962 – Warner Bros.
85 minutes – black and white
Producer: Bryan Foy. Director: Walter Doniger, Crane Wilbur. Screenplay: Crane Wilbur. Music: Howard Jackson. Editor: Leo H. Shreve. Make-up: Gordon Bau, Lou LaCava. Photography: Harold Stine. Sound: Robert B. Lee.

Cast: Shirley Knight *(Erica Hayden)*; Andrew Duggan *(Warden Frank Cole)*; Constance Ford *(Sophie Brice)*; **Barbara Nichols** *(Candy Kane)*; Margaret Hayes *(Zoe Stoughton)*; Jeanne Cooper *(Helen Jennings)*; Virginia Gregg *(Mrs. Edith Hunter)*; Patricia Huston *(Doris Jones)*; Jason Evers *(Dr. Conrad)*; Jennifer Howard *(Addie Gates)*; Caroline Richter *(Clemens)*; Gayla Graves *(Jackie Lynch)*; Colette Jackson *(Aggie)*; Jeanne Carmen *(Inmate)*.

The World of Henry Orient
1964 – United Artists
106 minutes – color
Producer: Jerome Hillman. Director: George Roy Hill. Screenplay: Nora Johnson, Nunnally Johnson, based on the novel by Nora Johnson. Music: Elmer Bernstein. Editor: Stuart Gilmore. Make-up: Dick

Smith. Photography: Boris Kaufman, Arthur J. Ornitz. Sound: Gilbert Marchant.

Cast: Peter Sellers *(Henry Orient)*; Paula Prentiss *(Stella Dunnworthy)*; Angela Lansbury *(Isabel Boyd)*; Tom Bosley *(Frank Boyd)*; Phyllis Thaxter *(Mrs. Avis Gilbert)*; Bibi Osterwald *(Erica 'Boothy' Booth)*; Merrie Spaeth *(Marian 'Gil' Gilbert)*; Tippy Walker *(Valarie 'Val' Campbell Boyd)*; John Fiedler *(Sidney)*; Al Lewis *(Store Owner)*; Peter Duchin *(Joe Daniels)*; Fred Stewart *(Doctor)*; Philippa Bevans *(Emma Hambler)*; Jane Buchanan *(Lillian Kafritz)*.

Looking for Love
1964 – MGM
85 minutes – color

Producer: Joe Pasternak. Director: Don Weis. Screenplay: Ruth Brooks Flippen. Music: George Stoll, Robert Van Eps. Editor: Adrienne Fazan. Make-up: William Tuttle. Photography: Milton Krasner. Sound: Conrad Kahn.

Cast: Connie Francis *(Libby Caruso)*; Jim Hutton *(Paul Davis)*; Susan Oliver *(Jan McNair)*; Joby Baker *(Cuz Rickover)*; **Barbara Nichols** *(Gaye Swinger)*; Johnny Carson *(Himself)*; George Hamilton *(Himself)*; Yvette Mimieux *(Herself)*; Paula Prentiss *(Herself)*; Danny Thomas *(Himself)*; Charles Lane *(Screen Test Director)*; Joan Marshall *(Miss Devine)*; Jesse White *(Tiger Shay)*; Jay C. Flippen *(Ralph Front)*; Bara Byrnes *(Miss LaRobe)*; Chris Noel *(Actress)*.

Dear Heart
1964 – Warner Bros.
114 minutes – black and white

Producer: Martin Manulis. Director: Delbert Mann. Screenplay: Tad Mosel. Music: Henry Mancini. Editor: Folmar Blangsted. Make-up: Gordon Bau. Photography: Russell Harlan. Sound: Robert B. Lee.

Cast: Glenn Ford *(Harry Mork)*; Geraldine Page *(Evie Jackson)*; Angela Lansbury *(Phyllis)*; Michael Anderson Jr. *(Patrick)*; **Barbara Nichols** *(June Loveland)*; Patricia Barry *(Mitchell)*; Charles Drake *(Frank Taylor)*; Richard Deacon *(Mr. Cruikshank)*; Neva Patterson *(Connie Templeton)*; Ken Lymch *(The Masher)*; Ruth McDevitt *(Miss Tait)*; Alice Pearce *(Miss Moore)*; Mary Wickes *(Miss Fox)*; Joanna Crawford *(Emile Zola Bernkrant)*; Peter Turgeon *(Peterson)*.

The Disorderly Orderly

1964 – Paramount

90 minutes – color

Producer: Paul Jones. Director: Frank Tashlin. Screenplay: Frank Tashlin, based on a story by Norm Liebman and Ed Haas. Music: Joseph J. Lilley. Editor: Russell Wiles, John Woodcock. Make-up: Bud Bashaw Jr., Jack Stone. Photography: W. Wallace Kelley. Sound: Don Merritt, Jim Miller, Bud Parman.

Cast: Jerry Lewis *(Jerome Littlefield)*; Glenda Farrell *(Dr. Jean Howard)*; Susan Oliver *(Susan Andrews)*; Karen Sharpe *(Julie Blair)*; Kathleen Freeman *(Nurse Maggie Higgins)*; Everett Sloane *(Mr. Tuffington)*; Del Moore *(Dr. Davenport)*; Alice Pearce *(Mrs. Fuzzibee)*; **Barbara Nichols** *(Miss Marlowe)*; Milton Frome *(Board Member)*; John Macchia *(Orderly)*; Jack E. Leonard *(Fat Jack)*; Muriel Landers *(Millicent)*; Frank Scannell *(Milton M. Mealy)*; Francine York *(Nurse)*.

The Human Duplicators

1965 – Woolner Bros.

100 minutes – color

Producer: Hugo Grimaldi, Arthur C. Pierce. Director: Hugo Grimaldi, Arthur C. Pierce. Screenplay: Arthur C. Pierce. Music: Gordon Zahler, Igo Kantor. Editor: Donald Wolfe. Make-up: Bob Mark. Photography: Monroe Askins. Sound: Robert Reeve.

Cast: George Nader *(Glenn Martin);* **Barbara Nichols** *(Gale Wilson);* George Macready *(Professor Vaughn Dornheimer);* Dolores Faith *(Lisa Dornheimer);* Hugh Beaumont *(Austin Welles);* Richard Arlen *(Lieutenant Shaw);* Richard Kiel *(Dr. Kolos);* John Indrisano *(Thor, the Butler);* Ted Durant *(The Galaxy Being);* Alean 'Bambi' Hamilton *(Brunette Lab Assistant);* Margaret Teele *(Blonde Lab Assistant);* Lori Lyons *(Miss Hart);* Walter Abel *(Dr. Munson).*

The Loved One
1965 – MGM
122 minutes – black and white
Producer: John Calley, Haskell Wexler. Director: Tony Richardson. Screenplay: Terry Southern, Christopher Isherwood, based on the novel Evelyn Waugh. Music: John Addison. Editor: Hal Ashby, Brian Smedley-Aston. Make-up: Emil La Vigne. Photography: Haskell Wexler. Sound: Stan Fiferman.
Cast: Robert Morse *(Dennis Barlow);* Jonathan Winters *(Henry Glenworthy/ Reverend Wilbur Glenworthy);* Anjanette Comer *(Aimee Thanatogenous);* Dana Andrews *(General Buck Brrinkman);* Milton Burke *(Mr. Kenton);* James Coburn *(Immigration Officer);* John Gielgud *(Sir Francis Hinsley);* Tab Hunter *(Whispering Glades Tour Guide);* Margaret Leighton *(Mrs. Helen Kenton);* Liberace *(Mr. Starker);* Roddy McDowall *(D.J. Jr.);* Robert Morley *(Sir Ambrose Ambercrombie);* **Barbara Nichols** *(Sadie Blodgett);* Dort Clark *(Colonel Burt).*

The Swinger
1966 – Paramount
81 minutes – color
Producer: George Sidney. Director: George Sidney. Screenplay: Lawrence Roman. Music: Marty Paich. Editor: Frank Santillo. Make-up: Wally Westmore. Photography: Joseph F. Biroc. Sound: Charles Grenzbach, Garry A. Harris.

Cast: Ann-Margret *(Kelly Olsson)*; Anthony Franciosa *(Ric Colby)*; Robert Coote *(Sir Hubert Charles)*; Yvonne Romain *(Karen Charles)*; Horace McMahon *(Detective Sergeant Hooker)*; Nydia Westman *(Aunt Cora)*; Craig Hill *(Sammy Jenkins)*; Milton Frome *(Mr. Olsson)*; **Barbara Nichols** *(Blossom La Tour)*; Myrna Ross *(Sally)*; Bert Freed *(Police Captain)*; Romo Vincent *(Jack Happy)*; Larry D. Mann *(John Mallory)*; Lance LeGault *(Warren)*; Diki Lerner *(Svengali)*.

The Power
1968 – MGM
108 minutes – color

Producer: George Pal. Directed by: Byron Haskin. Screenplay: John Gay, based on the novel by Frank M. Robinson. Music: Miklos Rozsa. Editor: Thomas J. McCarthy. Make-up: William Tuttle. Photography: Ellsworth Fredericks. Sound: Frank Milton.

Cast: George Hamilton *(Professor Jim Tanner)*; Suzanne Pleshette *(Professor Margery Lansing)*; Richard Carlson *(Professor Norman E. Van Zandt)*; Yvonne De Carlo *(Mrs. Sally Hallson)*; Earl Holliman *(Professor Talbot Scott)*; Gary Merrill *(Mark Corlane)*; Ken Murray *(Grover)*; **Barbara Nichols** *(Flora)*; Aldo Ray *(Bruce)*; Arthur O'Çonnell *(Professor Henry Hallson)*; Nehemiah Persoff *(Professor Carl Melnicker)*; Michael Rennie *(Arthur Nordlund)*.

Sette Uomini e un Cervello
1968 – Chiara Film Internazionali
106 minutes – color

Producer: Rossano Brazzi, Oscar Brazzi, Oscar Neguemnor, Juan Luis Rechaux, Alfredo Rádice. Director: Rossano Brazzi. Screenplay: Rossano Brazzi, Sandro Continenza, Marcello Coscia, based on a story by Rossano Brazzi. Music: Carlo Rustichelli. Editor: Giampiero Giunti. Make-up: Franco Corridoni. Photography: Stelvio Massi, Ricardo Younis. Sound: Bruno Borghi, José Castellanos, Leopodo Rosi.

Cast: Ann-Margret *(Leticia)*; Rossano Brazzi *(Ross Simpson)*; **Barbara Nichols** *(Secretary)*; Helene Chanel *(Georgette)*; Gina Maria Hidalgo *(Ana Veronesi)*; Osvaldo Pacheco *(Jose)*; Rafael Carret *(Antonio)*; Alberto Dalbes *(Schwartz)*; Lando Buzzanca *(Esteban de Flori)*; Roger Smith; Mimma Biscardi; Juan Carlos Lamas; Javier Portales; Alfonso Selvatore.

Charley and the Angel
1973 – Walt Disney Productions
93 minutes – color
Producer: Bill Anderson. Director: Vincent McEveety. Screenplay: Roswell Rogers, based on the novel *The Golden Evenings of Summer* by Will Stanton. Music: Buddy Baker. Editor: Bob Bring, Ray de Leuw. Make-up: Robert J. Schiffer. Photography: Charles F. Wheeler. Sound: Herb Taylor.
Cast: Fred MacMurray *(Charles Appleby)*; Cloris Leachman *(Nettie Appleby)*; Harry Morgan *(The Angel formerly Roy Zerney)*; Kurt Russell *(Ray Ferris)*; Kathleen Cody *(Leonora Appleby)*; Vincent Van Patten *(Willie Appleby)*; Scott Kolden *(Rupert Appleby)*; George Lindsey *(Pete)*; Edward Andrews *(Ernie)*; Richard Bakalyan *(Buggs)*; **Barbara Nichols** *(Sadie)*; Kelly Thordsen *(Policeman)*; Liam Dunn *(Dr. Sprague)*; Larry D. Mann *(Felix)*.

The Photographer
1974 – AVCO Embassy Pictures
94 minutes – color
Producer: William Byron Hillman. Director: William Byron Hillman. Screenplay: William Byron Hillman. Music: Jack Goga. Editor: Tony de Zarraga. Make-up: Jerry Soucie. Photography: Mike Shea. Sound: Gregory Dillon.
Cast: Michael Callan *(Adrian Wilde)*; **Barbara Nichols** *(Mrs. Wilde)*; Harold J. Stone *(Lieutenant Luther Jacoby)*; Edward Andrews *(Sergeant Sid Collins)*; Jed Allan *(Joe Hennesey)*; Spencer Milligan *(Clinton Webber)*; Susan Damante *(Quinn Lovette)*; Liv Lindeland *(Mrs. Fowler)*; Patty

Bodeen *(Candy Fain)*; Betty Anne Rees *(Karri Stephenson)*; Jennifer Leak *(Elowise Atkins)*; Ronda Copland *(Lisa Tuttle)*; Isabel Sanford *(Mrs. Slade)*.

Won Ton Ton, the Dog Who Saved Hollywood

1976 – Paramount

92 minutes – color

Producer: David V. Picker, Arnold Schulman, Michael Winner. Director: Michael Winner. Screenplay: Arnold Schulman, Cy Howard. Music: Neal Hefti. Editor: Bernard Gribble. Make-up: Philip Rhodes. Photography: Richard H. Kline. Sound: Terence Rawlings.

Cast: Bruce Dern *(Grayson Potchuck)*; Madeline Kahn *(Estie Del Ruth)*; Art Carney *(J. J. Fromberg)*; Phil Silvers *(Murry Fromberg)*; Teri Garr *(Fluffy Peters)*; Ron Leibman *(Rudy Montague)*; Virginia Mayo *(Miss Battley)*; Rory Calhoun *(Philip Hart)*; Ethel Merman *(Hedda Parsons)*; Nancy Walker *(Mrs. Fromberg)*; Rhonda Fleming *(Rhoda Flaming)*; Dean Stockwell *(Paul Lavell)*; Tab Hunter *(David Hamilton)*; Victor Mature *(Nick)*; **Barbara Nichols** *(Nick's Girl)*.

Manfish. Barbara, Vincent Chang, Tessa Prendergast and Lon Chaney.

Miracle in the Rain.

The Wild Party. Jay Robinson, Anthony Quinn, Arthur Franz, Barbara and Paul Stewart.

Beyond a Reasonable Doubt.

The King and Four Queens. Barbara, Jo Van Fleet, Sara Shane and Jean Willes.

Sweet Smell of Success. Barbara and Tony Curtis.

The Pajama Game.

FILMOGRAPHY

Pal Joey. Barbara and Frank Sinatra.

Ten North Frederick. Barbara and Gary Cooper.

The Naked and the Dead. Barbara and Aldo Ray.

That Kind of Woman. Barbara and Jack Warden.

Woman Obsessed. Stephen Boyd, Barbara and James Philbrook.

The Scarface Mob. Barbara and Neville Brand.

Who Was That Lady? Barbara and Tony Curtis.

Where the Boys Are.

The George Raft Story.

House of Women.

The World of Henry Orient. Barbara and Peter Sellers.

Looking for Love. Barbara and Jim Hutton.

Dear Heart. Barbara and Angela Lansbury and Glenn Ford.

The Disorderly Orderly. Barbara and Jerry Lewis.

The Human Duplicators. Barbara and George Nader.

The Loved One. Barbara and Robert Morse.

The Swinger. Barbara and Ann Margret.

The Power. Barbara and George Hamilton.

Charley and the Angel. Fred MacMurray, Pat Delaney and Barbara in the background.

(Courtesy of Janice Pease).

Television Appearances

1951
Broadway Open House: NBC, Barbara Nichols *(Agathon)*.
Chesterfield Sound Off Time: NBC, Barbara Nichols *(Agathon)*.

1952
Stage Entrance: DuMont Television Network,
Barbara Nichols *(Secretary Taffy Tuttle)*.

1953
Studio One: CBS – November 30. "Confessions of a Nervous Man." Barbara Nichols *(First Pretty Girl)*.

1954

The Mask: CBS – January 10, "Murder in the Burlesque House." Barbara Nichols *(Burlesque Dancer).*

The United States Steel Hour: ABC – June 8. "Good for You." Barbara Nichols *(Bridie).*

The Philco Television Playhouse: NBC – August 8. "The Man in the Middle of the Ocean."
Barbara Nichols *(Ruth).*

Center Stage: ABC – September 21. "Heart of a Clown"

Armstrong Circle Theatre: NBC – November 9. "Fred Allen's Sketchbook." Barbara Nichols *(Bar Patron / Party Flirt / Bobsey Baxter).*

1955

Caesar's Hour. NBC. Barbara Nichols *(Rosalie).*

Danger: CBS – April 12. "Sandy River Blues." Barbara Nichols *(Scheherazade).*

Caesar Presents Comedy Preview: NBC – July 4. Barbara Nichols *(Barbara Williams).*

1956

It's a Great Life: NBC – March 25. "Glamour Doll." Barbara Nichols *(Caroline Cabot).*

The Bob Cummings Show: CBS – April 5. "The Con Man." Barbara Nichols *(Sheila).*

It's a Great Life: NBC – April 15. "The Return of Caroline." Barbara Nichols *(Caroline Cabot).*

Chevron Hall of Stars: Four Star – November 22. "Double Cross." Barbara Nichols *(Rosie).*

1957
Blondie: NBC – April 5. "The Glamour Girl. Barbara Nichols *(Vivian Valentine).*

Toast of the Town – The Ed Sullivan Show. (The Ninth Anniversary Show). CBS – June 23.
Barbara Nichols *(Herself).*

Tabloid: CBC – July 3. Barbara Nichols *(Herself).*

The Steve Allen Show: NBC – September 29. Barbara Nichols *(Herself).*

Matinee Theatre: NBC – December 19. "Gentleman Caller"

The Thin Man: NBC – December 27. "Unwelcome Alibi." Barbara Nichols *(Jeri).*

1958
Maverick: ABC – January 5. "The Third Rider." Barbara Nichols *(Blanche).*

Love that Jill: ABC – January 20. "Tonight's the Night." Barbara Nichols *(Ginger).*

Love that Jill: ABC – January 27. "The Mating Machine." Barbara Nichols *(Ginger).*

Love that Jill ABC – February 3. "Who Done It?" Barbara Nichols *(Ginger)*.

Love that Jill ABC – February 10. "They Went Thataway." Barbara Nichols *(Ginger)*.

Love that Jill ABC – February 17. "Vote for Me Darling." Barbara Nichols *(Ginger)*.

Love that Jill ABC – February 24. "Operation Double Cross." Barbara Nichols *(Ginger)*.

Love that Jill ABC – March 3. "Kiss Me Sergeant." Barbara Nichols *(Ginger)*.

Love that Jill ABC – March 10. "Hug Hat Hillbilly." Barbara Nichols *(Ginger)*.

Love that Jill ABC – March 17. "Kid Stuff." Barbara Nichols *(Ginger)*.

Love that Jill ABC – March 24. "Two for the Money." Barbara Nichols *(Ginger)*.

Love that Jill ABC – March 31. "Bess of the Bowery." Barbara Nichols *(Ginger)*.

Love that Jill ABC – April 5. "Love That Foreign Sports Car." Barbara Nichols *(Ginger)*.

The Red Skelton Show CBS – April 8. "Bolivar Gets Amnesia." Barbara Nichols *(Gertie, Bolivar's Girlfriend)*.

Love that Jill ABC – April 14. "Make Mine Marriage." Barbara Nichols *(Ginger)*.

Shower of Stars CBS – April 17. Barbara Nichols *(Miss Kim O'Day)*.

Climax! CBS – May 29. "The Push-Button Giant." Barbara Nichols *(Gale Benson)*.

Tonight starring Jack Paar NBC – July 11. Barbara Nichols *(Herself)*.

The Steve Lawrence-Eydie Gormé Show NBC – August 24. Barbara Nichols *(Herself)*.

The Bob Cummings Show CBS – September 23. "Bob and Schultzy Reunite." Barbara Nichols *(Marian Billington)*.

The Bob Cummings Show CBS – September 30. "Bob and the Dumb Blonde." Barbara Nichols *(Marian Billington)*.

Dragnet NBC – October 7. "The Big Star." Barbara Nichols

The Red Skelton Show CBS – October 14. "Bolivar – the Quiz Champ." Barbara Nichols *(Gertie, Bolivar's Girlfriend)*.

The Milton Berle Show NBC – November 19. Barbara Nichols *(Herself / Receptionist)*.

The Jack Benny Program CBS – December 28. "Christmas Gift Exchange" Barbara Nichols *(Mildred Meyerhouser)*.

1959

The Thin Man NBC – January 9. "The Case of the Baggy Pants." Barbara Nichols *(Stripper Ritta Fayne)*.

Westinghouse Desilu Playhouse CBS – April 20. "The Untouchables: Part 1." Barbara Nichols *(Brandy La France).*

Westinghouse Desilu Playhouse CBS – April 27. "The Untouchables: Part 2." Barbara Nichols *(Brandy La France).*

The Real McCoys ABC – October 9. "The Politician." Barbara Nichols *(Gladys Slade).*

The Untouchables ABC – October 15. "The Empty Chair." Barbara Nichols *(Barbara Ritchie / Brandy La France).*

The Jack Benny Program CBS – November 15. "The Jimmy Stewart Show." Barbara Nichols *(Mildred Meyerhouser).*

The Dennis O'Keefe Show CBS – November 24. "There Goes the Groom." Barbara Nichols *(Gold Digging Showgirl).*

The Red Skelton Show CBS – December 8. "Bolivar the Songwriter." Barbara Nichols *(Myrtle, Bolivar's Girlfriend).*

1960

The Red Skelton Show CBS – February 23. "Bolivar and the Roaring Twenties." Barbara Nichols *(Gertie, Bolivar's Girlfriend).*

The Jack Benny Program CBS – April 17. "Easter Show." Barbara Nichols *(Mildred Meyerhouser).*

Here's Hollywood November 15. Barbara Nichols *(Herself).*

Stagecoach West ABC – November 15. "A Time to Run." Barbara Nichols *(Sadie Wren).*

The Jack Benny Program CBS – December 11. "Jack Goes to a Concert." Barbara Nichols *(Mildred Meyerhouser)*.

1961

March of Dimes - What About Linda? January 14. Barbara Nichols *(Herself)*.

The Twilight Zone CBS – February 10. "Twenty Two." Barbara Nichols *(Liz Powell)*.

General Electric Theater CBS – March 12. "The Small Elephants." Barbara Nichols *(Leslie Blaine)*.

Michael Shayne NBC – March 31. "Marriage Can Be Fatal." Barbara Nichols *(Topaz McQueen)*.

The Detectives ABC – May 12. "Duty Date." Barbara Nichols *(Abby Landis)*.

Miami Undercover United Artists TV – May 22. "Kitty." Barbara Nichols *(Kitty)*.

Westinghouse Playhouse NBC – June 16. "House Guest." Barbara Nichols *(Lorraine Hadley)*.

1962

Pantomime Quiz - Stump the Stars CBS – November 19. Barbara Nichols *(Herself / Guest Panelist)*.

The Dick Powell Show NBC – April 24. "No Strings Attached" Barbara Nichols *(Bunny Easter)*.

1963

Alcoa Premiere ABC – January 24. "Five, Six, Pick Up Sticks." Barbara Nichols *(Willy Simms)*.

Going My Way ABC – February 20. "Has Anyone Seen Eddie?" Barbara Nichols *(Marie)*.

Vacation Playhouse CBS – September 2. "All About Barbara." Barbara Nichols *(Barbara Adams)*.

Arrest and Trial ABC – September 22. "Isn't it a Lovely View." Barbara Nichols *(Ginny)*.

The Tonight Show NBC – October 18. Barbara Nichols *(Herself)*.

The Beverly Hillbillies CBS – October 30. "Jethro's First Love." Barbara Nichols *(Chickadee Laverne)*.

Grindl NBC – November 3. "Grindl, Witness for the Defense." Barbara Nichols *(Wilma Bryan)*.

The Beverly Hillbillies CBS – November 6. "Chickadee Returns." Barbara Nichols *(Chickadee Laverne)*.

1964

Kraft Suspense Theatre NBC – February 6. "My Enemy, This Town." Barbara Nichols *(Ann Hilts)*.

The Travels of Jaimie McPheeters ABC – March 8. "The Day of the Dark Deeds." Barbara Nichols *(Mamie)*.

TELEVISION APPEARANCES

1965

Laredo NBC – October 28. "A Question of Discipline." Barbara Nichols *(Princess)*.

1966

The Wild Wild West CBS – February 18. "The Night of the Whirring End." Barbara Nichols *(Bessie)*.

Batman ABC – September 7. "Shoot a Crooked Arrow." Barbara Nichols *(Maid Marilyn)*.

Batman ABC – September 8. "Walk the Straight and Narrow. Barbara Nichols *(Maid Marilyn)*.

1967

Green Acres CBS – February 8. "Never Take Your Wife to a Convention." Barbara Nichols *(Wanda)*.

The Girl from U.N.C.L.E. NBC – March 14. "The Phi Beta Killer Affair." Barbara Nichols *(Ida Martz)*.

The Tonight Show CBS – July. Barbara Nichols *(Herself)*.

The Jackie Gleason Show CBS – November 18. "The Honeymooners: Two Faces of Ralph Kramden." Barbara Nichols *(Kitty, Big Sam's Moll)*.

1968

The Merv Griffin Show CBS – April 16. Barbara Nichols *(Herself)*.

1969

Hawaii Five-O CBS – September 24. "A Thousand Pardons – You're Dead!" Barbara Nichols *(Betsy)*.

1971

The Smith Family ABC – April 21. "Greener Pastures." Barbara Nichols *(Effie)*.

Adam-12 NBC – November 3. "Truant." Barbara Nichols *(Ginger Stephens)*.

The Doris Day Show CBS – November 8. "Have I Got a Fellow for You!" Barbara Nichols *(Mrs. Hollister)*.

Love, American Style ABC – December 31. "Love and the Doctor's Honeymoon." Barbara Nichols *(Gladys)*.

1972

Adam-12 NBC – November 22. "The Vendetta." Barbara Nichols *(Janice Walker)*.

1973

Adam-12 NBC – October 3. "West Valley Division." Barbara Nichols *(Elizabeth Mitchell)*.

1974

Emergency! NBC – December 7. "Details." Barbara Nichols *(Ginger)*.

The Rookies ABC – December 16. "Blue Christmas." Barbara Nichols *(Marie Antoinette)*.

1975

Medical Story NBC – October 9. "An Air Full of Death." Barbara Nichols *(Mrs. Fondaris)*.

Good for You. Barbara, Orson Bean and Diana Lynn, 1954.

Heart of a Clown, 1954. (Courtesy of Janice Pease).

It's a Great Life. Barbara and James Dunn, 1956.

Blondie. Barbara, Arthur Lake and Pamela Britton, 1957.

Bolivar - The Quiz Champ. Barbara and Red Skelton, 1958.

Bolivar Gets Amnesia. Barbara, Red Skelton and Lynn Bari, 1958.

Television Appearances

Love That Jill. Barbara and Robert Sterling, 1958.

The Bob Cummings Show. Barbara, Bob Cummings and Ann B. Davis, 1958.

The Jack Benny Program, 1958.

The Case of the Baggy Pants. Barbara and Peter Lawford, 1959.

Television Appearances

The Jack Benny Program, 1959.

The Real McCoys. Barbara and Walter Brennan, 1959.

The Untouchables. Barbara, Joe Mantell and Bill Williams, 1959.

The Small Elephants. Barbara and Cliff Robertson, 1961.

TELEVISION APPEARANCES

All About Barbara. Barbara and William Bishop, 1963.

Five, Six, Pick Up Sticks. Barbara, Mickey Rooney and John Forsythe, 1963.

Going My Way. Barbara and Gene Nelson, 1963.

My Enemy, This Town. Barbara and Scott Marlowe, 1964.

Laredo. Barbara and Barbara Werle, 1965.

Batman. Barbara and Art Carney, 1966.

Emergency! Barbara and Julie London, 1974.

Magazine Covers

Picture Post, June 12 1948. (United Kingdom).

Front Page Detective, December 1948.

Master Detective, February 1949.

Sir! March 1949. (Courtesy of James Krajewski).

Federal Detective Bureau, October 1950. (Courtesy of James Krajewski).

Front Page Detective, November 1950.

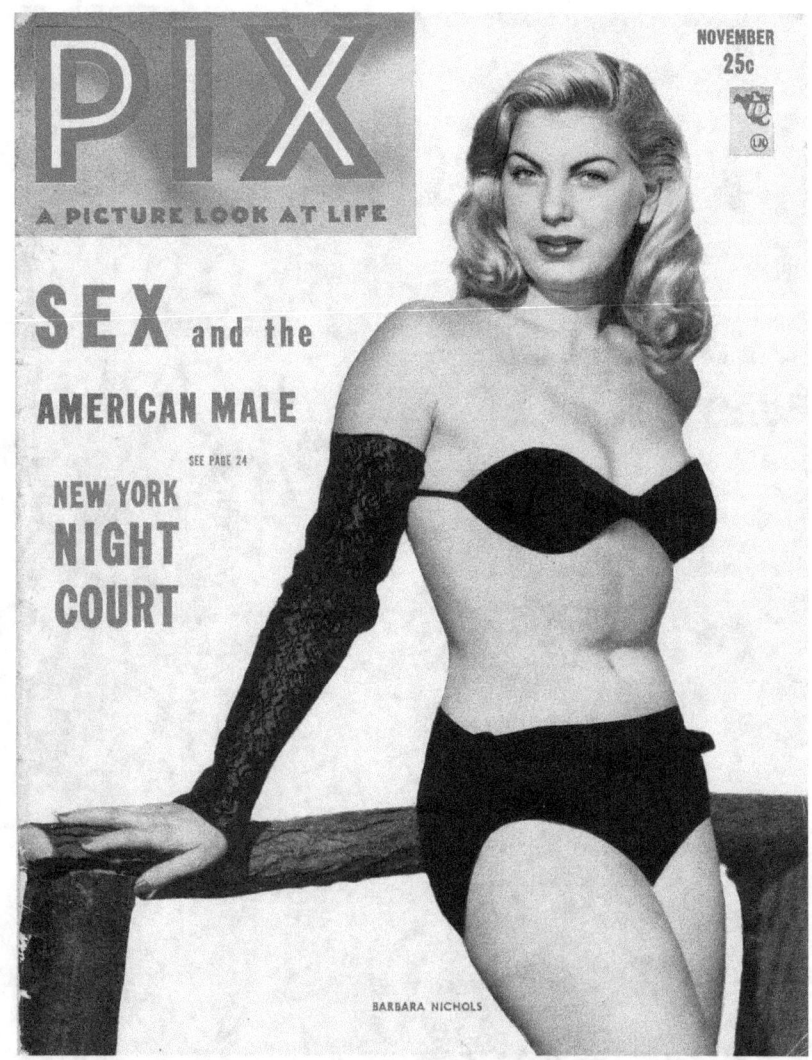

Pix, November 1950.

Headquarters Detective, November 1950.

Man to Man, May 1951.

Startling Detective, September 1951. (Courtesy of James Krajewski).

Uncensored Detective, September 1951. (Courtesy of James Krajewski).

Art Photography, October 1951.

Man to Man, November 1952. (Courtesy of James Krajewski).

Gala, January 1953.

Fact Detective Yearbook, 1954.

TV Guide, June 25-July 1 1955.

Paris Frou Frou, 1956 (France).

Modern Man, September 1956.

Sir! January 1957.

Gala, January 1957.

Visto, February 9 1957. (Italy).

Mascotte, August 28 1957. (Italy).

New York News Sunday, September 15, 1957.

Paris Frou Frou, 1958. (France).

ABC Film Review, October 1958. (United Kingdom).

MAGAZINE COVERS

Blighty Parade, October 24 1959. (United Kingdom).

People Today, August 1960.

Cinémonde, January 10 1961. (France).

Bibliography

Bernard, Susan. *Bernard of Hollywood – The Ultimate Pin-up Book.* Cologne: Taschen, 2002.

Buford, Kate. *Burt Lancaster: An American Life.* New York: Random House, Inc., 2000.

Cameron, Ian and Elisabeth. *Dames.* New York: Frederick A. Praeger, Inc., Publishers, 1969.

Holley, Val. *Mike Connolly and the Manly Art of Hollywood Gossip*. Jefferson: McFarland & Company, Inc., 2003.

Hunter, Tab with Muller, Eddie. *Tab Hunter Confidential – The Making of a Movie Star*. New York: Algonquin Books of Chapel Hill, 2006.

James, Brando. *Jeanne Carmen – My Wild, Wild Life*. Lincoln: iUniverse, Inc., 2006.

Kleno, Larry. *Kim Novak on Camera*. New York: A.S. Barnes & Company, Inc., 1980.

Koper, Richard. *Fifties Blondes – Sexbombs, Sirens, Bad Girls and Teen Queens*. The BearManor Media: Duncan, Oklahoma, 2010.

Krasna, Norman. *Who Was That Lady I Saw You With?* New York: Random House, 1958.

McBain, Diane and Michaud, Michael Gregg. *Famous Enough – A Hollywood Memoir*. The BearManor Media: Duncan, Oklahoma, 2014.

Terrace, Vincent. *Encyclopedia of Television Pilots 1937-2012*. Jefferson: McFarland & Company, Inc., 2013.

Van Doren, Mamie. *Playing the Field – Sex, Stardom, Love, and Life in Hollywood*. Newport Beach, CA: Starlet Suave Books, 2013.

Vecchio, Deborah Del. *Beverly Garland – Her Life and Career*. Jefferson: McFarland & Company, Inc., 2013.

Index

Andrews, Dana — 78, 79, *91*, 94, 283, 292.
Andrews, Eddie — *277*, 294.
Angelich, Lauren — 254.
Ann Margret — 249, 251, 293, 294, *319*.
Arnaz, Desi — xxi, 170.
Archerd, Army — *xxxiii*.
Avalon, Frankie — 247, 248, *255*.
Axelrod, George — 59.
Bacall, Lauren — 18, 217.
Bacharach, Burt — 219.
Ball, Lucille — 170, 219.
Bari, Lynn — 175, *338*.
Basch, Peter — 34, 57, 58.
Bean, Orson — *333*.
Beaumont, Hugh — 232, *243*, 292.
Benny, Jack — xx, 174, 175, *182*, 288, 327 – 329, *341*, *343*.
Best, James — 138, 286.
Bikel, Theodore — *179*, 287.
Binns, Edward — *88*, 283.

Bishop, Joey	*146*, 251, 286.
Bishop, William	*347*.
Blau, Bruce	20, 21, 250.
Bouvard, Robert	247.
Boyd, Stephen	170, 171, *178*, 287, *307*.
Brand, Neville	235, *308*.
Brando, Marlon	204.
Brennan, Walter	*344*.
Britton, Pamela	*336*.
Byrnes, Edd	204.
Caesar, Sid	74-76, 135, 324.
Carmen, Jeanne	97, 202, 289.
Carpenter, John	3, 22, 169
Carney, Art	59, 249, 295, *352*.
Carson, Johnny	228, 250, 251, 290.
Carter, Jack	60, *69*, 219, 267.
Chaney Jr., Lon	61, 71, 282, *296*
Chang, Vincent	282, *296*.
Chase, Barrie	205, 206, 285, 289.
Cochran, Steve	60, 61, *68*, 73, 76, 168.
Cody, Kathleen	264, 265, 294.
Cohan, John	4, 57, 124, 125, 168, 189, 201, 202, 204, 207, 218, 221, 230, 270.
Connolly, Mike	110, 140, 156, 249,
Cooper, Gary	*xxxi*, 137, 138, *144*, 286, *304*.
Corridoni, Franco	251, 293.
Cox, Elaine	18.
Crosby, Gary	*274*.
Cummings, Bob	170, 324, 327, *340*.
Curtis, Tony	108, 109, *115*, *116*, 185, 186, 188, 190, *193*, 284, 288, 301, *309*.
Dagmar	37, 38, 124, 125.
Dante, Michael	136.
Danton, Ray	205, *213*, 289.
Davis, Ann B.	*340*.
Day, Doris	74, 106, *111*, *112*, 285, 332.
De Carlo, Yvonne	140, 247, 252, *255*, 267, 293.
Delaney, Pat	*321*.
Dickinson, Angie	220, *224*.
Dienes, Andre de	34.
Donahue, Troy	204, 207.
Doniger, Walter	202, *208*, 289.
Drummond, Dee	20, 21, *29*, 32, 250.
Druxman, Michael B.	60, 264.
Dunn, James	335.
Eames, CeCe	32, 33.
Ebsen, Buddy	*225*.

Egan, Richard	*69*.
Elhardt, Kaye	*143*.
Fitzpatrick, Tom	18, 19.
Flagg, James Montgomery	34.
Flippen, Jay C.	*241*, 284, 290.
Ford, Constance	204, 207, *209*, *210*, 289.
Ford, Glenn	228, *237*, *238*, 270, 291, *315*.
Ford, Peter	229, 248.
Forsythe, John	222, *348*.
Foster, Phil	75.
Foy Jr., Eddie	*111*, 285.
Francis, Connie	189, *196*, 201, 202, 229, 230, *241*, 288, 290.
Franz, Arthur	283, *298*.
Gable, Clark	78, 93 – 97, *99 – 101*, 140, 185, 235, 284.
Gabor, Zsa Zsa	123, 221, 251.
Garland, Beverly	221.
Gibson, Mimi	xxi.
Girosi, Marcello	*158*, 286.
Gobel, George	217 – 219.
Grable, Betty	18, 217, 267.
Hadley, Nancy	*143*.
Hamilton, George	*196*, 252, 288, 290, 293, *320*.
Hargitay, Mickey	125.
Harlow, Jean	xi, 140.
Hart, Dolores	*196*, 288.
Hathaway, Henry	171, 287.
Hauser, Gretchen	32.
Hawn, Goldie	248.
Hayward, Susan	170, 171, *177*, 287.
Hill, James	108, 110, 284.
Hillman, William B.	xxii, 266, 267, 294.
Holliday, Judy	59, 60.
Holmes, Dennis	171, *177*, 287.
Hopper, Hedda	18, 33, 110, 140,
Hughes, Kathleen	60.
Hunter, Tab	xx, 151 – 154, *159*, *160*, *163*, 229, 267, 268, 286, 292, 295.
Hutton, Jim	*195*, *196*, 229, *241*, 288, 290, *314*.
Janis, Conrad	76, 77.
Johnson, Van	74, 75, *82*, 282.
Kaplan, Marvin	190.
Kelly, Claire	*143*.
Kennedy, Robert	221.
King, Alan	74, 75, *82*, 282.
Knight, Shirley	202 – 204, *208*, *209*, 289.
Kollmar, Richard	31 – 33.
Lake, Arthur	*336*.

Lamarr, Hedy	221.
Lancaster, Burt	108 – 110, *119*, 140, 284.
Lane, Rusty	172, 173.
Lang, Fritz	78, 79, 283.
Lansbury, Angela	290, 291, *315*.
Lansing, Joi	94, 185, 187, *192*, *193*, 288.
Lawford, Peter	267, *342*.
Leigh, Janet	185, 186, 188, *193*, 288.
Lester, Jerry	37 – 39.
Lewis, Jerry	231, *241*, 291, *316*.
London, Julie	205, 289, *353*.
Loren, Sophia	58, 151 – 156, *158 – 163*, 286.
Loughery, Jackie	36.
Lumet, Sidney	151, 152, *158*, 286.
Luna, Barbara	252, 253.
Lynn, Diana	*333*.
MacLaine, Shirley	151.
MacMurray, Fred	264, 294, *321*.
Mann, Delbert	228, 290.
Mannix, Toni	57.
Mansfield, Jayne	xix, xx, 73, 77, 123 – 125, 135, 138, 172, 205, 217, 232, 234, 235, 289.
Mantell, Joe	287, *345*.
Markey, Doris	32.
Markey, Melinda	137.
Marlowe, Scott	229, *350*.
Marshall, Peter	*273*.
Martin, Dean	185, 186, 187, *193*, 288.
Martin, Quinn	170, 172, 287.
Marx, Harpo	*65*.
Mason, Marlyn	235.
Matteson, Rob	254.
Mature, Victor	267, *295*.
McBain, Diane	229.
Milner, Martin	274, 284.
Monroe, Marilyn	xix, xx, 34, 55, 58, 61, 77, 78, 80, 123 – 126, 137, 138, 154, 172, 190, 201, 205, 221, 265, 270, 281.
Moore, Al	39.
Moran, Earl	32, 34.
Morse, Robert	234, 292, *318*.
Nader, George	232, 233, *243*, 291, *317*.
Nelson, Gene	*349*.
Nickerauer, George	x, 1, 4, *9*, 98, 271.
Nickerauer – Wurst, Julia	1, *10*, 98, 269, 271, *279*.
Noonan, Tommy	77.
Norring, Ava	133 – 135.
Novak, Kim	121 – 123, *128*, 247, 285.

O'Neill, Lynne	249, 250, *258*, 267.
Ohmart, Carol	35, *41*, *42*, 76, 283.
Pall, Gloria	xviii, 36, 37, 175, 188.
Parker, Eleanor	78, 95, 96, *99*, 284.
Parsons, Louella	157.
Pease, Janice	6, 169, 207, 252.
Pelish, Thelma	*113*, 285.
Pero, Taylor	254.
Philbrook, James	287, *307*.
Pleshette, Suzanne	207, 252, 293.
Ponti, Carlo	151, 157, *158*, 286.
Powell, Dick	220, *224*, 329.
Prendergast, Tessa	62, 282, *296*.
Prentiss, Paula	*196*, 288, 289.
Price, Vincent	137.
Quinn, Anthony	76, 283, *298*.
Raft, George	205, *212*.
Raitt, John	106, *111*, 285.
Ray, Aldo	138, *147 – 149*, 252, 286, 293, 305.
Raymond, Robin	79, 80, *88*, 283.
Reeves, George	57.
Rennie, Michael	97, 252, 293.
Reynolds, Dean	*222*.
Riordan, Christopher	122, 206, 230, 234, 253, 263.
Robertson, Cliff	138, *149*, 190, 286, *346*.
Robinson, Jay	283, *298*.
Rodriguez, Santiago	251.
Rooney, Mickey	222, *348*.
Rubin, Stanley	58, 60, 281.
Russell, Ron	153 – 156.
St. Cyr, Lily	35, 139, *149*, 202, 286.
Sanders, George	152, 190, *198*, 286.
Sellers, Peter	227, 228, 290, *313*.
Shane, Sara	94, 96, 97, *99*, 284, *300*.
Sherwood, Gregg	35, *41*, *42*.
Sinatra, Frank	35, 121 – 123, *127*, *129*, *130*, 269, 285, *303*.
Skelton, Red	xx, 174, 175, 326 – 328, *337*, *338*.
Skolsky, Sidney	*xxix*, 76.
Smight, Jack	191.
Stack, Robert	172, *181*, 287.
Stanwyck, Barbara	201.
Sterling, Robert	136, *339*.
Stewart, Gloria	174, *182*.
Stewart, James	174, *182*.
Stewart, Paul	76, 283, *298*.
Stewart, Paula	60, 110, 217 – 219, 270.
Stone, Harold	*277*, 294.

Strait, Ray   125.
Straw, Jack   *113*, 285.
Talbot, Nita   *245*.
Teele, Margaret   232, 233, 292.
Thorne, Dyanne   187.
Van Doren, Mamie   xx, 124, 168, 220, *224*, 232, *273*.
Van Fleet, Jo   94 – 96, 284, *300*.
Vickers, Yvette   168.
Voorhees, Richard   169, *279*.
Walsh, Raoul   95 – 97, 284, 286.
Warden, Jack   153, 157, *159*, *161*, 286, *306*.
Wayne, Fredd   *199*.
Werle, Barbara   235, *351*.
West, Mae   35, 140, 168.
White, David   *117*.
Willes, Jean   94, 96, 97, *99*, 284, *300*.
Wilson, Earl   xxi, 18, 55, 97, 107, 123, 140, 175, 219, 233.
Williams, Bill   287, *345*.
Winters, Shelley   123, 202, 217.
Wyman, Frances   32.
Wynn, Keenan   157, *161*, 173, 286, 287.
Wynn, May   36.
Zappia, Bill   268, *279*.

www.ingramcontent.com/pod-product-compliance
Lightning Source LLC
Chambersburg PA
CBHW051828230426
43671CB00008B/875